# P⏻WER Moms

# Single Moms

Dr. Sherrie Walton & Co-Authors

Walton Publishing House,

Houston, Texas

www.iamsherriewalton.com


Printed in the United States of America

Disclaimer: The advice and strategies found within may not be suitable for every situation. This work is sold with the understanding that neither the author nor the publisher are held responsible for the results accrued from the advice in this book.

Library of Congress Cataloging-in-Publication Data has been applied for.

ISBN: 978-0-578-46561-6

# FOREWORD

This book is written in honor of the single mother who fearlessly takes on life with a persistence and power that cannot be matched or underestimated. As moms we often feel as if we aren't doing enough and that we are very uninformed about the true responsibility it takes to successfully raise children in today's world.

This book encompasses the stories of women from all different backgrounds: never married, divorced (twice), widowed, and remarried. Although they are all different, there is a common thread; they have fully embraced their lives and learned that the most important role they will ever have is a mother. A mother's love cannot be replaced. A mother's love transcends time and gets right to the point of their child's needs.

POWER Moms we need you… the world needs you… your children need you. It's probably not often you hear the words "Thank you," or "You're doing an amazing job." So, as you read through the pages of this book, it is our prayer that it encourages, motives, and empowers you to keep going.

There isn't one mother on the face of the earth who has felt she ever got it right. So as we salute the single moms throughout the pages of this book, we hope that you will rediscover and find your P.O.W.E.R.

Dr. Sherrie Walton

# Table of Contents

**Where do you find your POWER?**

I believe the women in my life helped me discover my power as a single mom, but I did not activate my power until my encounter with God. He showed me why I was created, and only then was I able to walk in the fullness of my power.

# CHAPTER 1

## THE G.I.R.L. IN THE MIRROR

### By Chassity Heard

—◈—

As I sit here writing in my apartment with my six-year-old daughter, I begin to question myself... *"How did you end up here?"* *"What are you doing with your life?"* All of these questions continue to make me doubt God and cause me to beat myself up mentally. Even though circumstances around me are is not how I planned them, I am closer to God than I have ever been. He is reintroducing me to myself and showing me that I AM **G**ifted, **I**ntelligent, **R**elevant, AND fear**L**ess! I am trusting Him to be my provider, my protector and, most of all, my husband during this season. Believe me; this has not always been the case.

In 2010, I remember standing in the bathroom holding a positive pregnancy test in my hand. I looked in the mirror feeling lost, disappointed, and just plain stupid! "How did I let this happen... again?" I asked myself. Yes, I said again. Let me rewind, so you can catch up. In 2005, I met a guy while I was working as a youth facilitator for a summer program at the University of Houston (U of

H). We were eating lunch at the same table with our group of kids, and he was talking to one of our co-workers. Of course, I was eavesdropping while I was eating.

I heard him say, "Yeah man… I just got out of jail last night, and my brother got me this job." *Wait… What? Did he just say jail!?!?* is what I thought. You know I started judging him, and immediately put him in the category of "OHN"—Oh, Hell Naw!—so when he'd start asking me questions about myself, I'd be able to answer with a wall up. My responses would be quick, short, and vague as in, "Sir, you do not need to know all of my business; you just got out of jail!"

The next day, we were on our way to take our group to do an activity, and out of nowhere one of the kids asked me, "Miss, do you have a boyfriend?" I turned around and yelled, "If he wants to know, he needs to ask me himself!" That was strike two for me, but wait… why was I even giving him strikes when he was supposed to be out to begin with? As you can see, I was low-key attracted to him. He was cute… dark-skinned with light brown eyes, and he had a nice build. Before the day ended, he respectably approached me, and we began to converse.

I soon discovered we actually took college Algebra together, and he had been watching me on campus for an entire year. As soon as he told me what I was wearing one day on campus, my wall was non-existent, and my heart was wide-open. I gave him my number, and from that day forward we were inseparable. I know what you're thinking… *What happened to him being in the category? Why is she ignoring all of these red flags?* I was a sucker for love. He was Bae!

I equated him showing interest in me as love. He was giving me

2

what I did not get from my dad or God. I attended church because it was the right thing to do, and I did not know a real relationship could exist with God. I knew Bae was the one, and you could not tell me differently. At the tender age of 19, I knew what was best for me, or so I thought. As the days turned into months, I began to see more red flags; yet, we had so much in common.

We both grew up in a single-parent home, and our fathers were in and out of our lives. We connected in pain, which made us love even harder. We would cling on to each other so tightly that it was actually suffocating our relationship. He had a two-year-old son and a broken baby mama to deal with. All of the dysfunction in his life lead him to smoke a lot. How many of you know that if you stay in an environment long enough, you will eventually become it? Yep; I began to smoke weed, experimented with X pills, and drank alcohol more than normal. As you can see, I got lost while trying to discover the woman I wanted to be. That season in my life reminded me so much of Eve in the garden. Eve was so determined to discover who she was, she was willing to do anything for it. Have you ever felt like you were lacking something? I'm not talking about lacking material or perishable things; I'm referring to the imperishable—you. *Who am I? Why was I born? What am I supposed to be doing with my life?* were my thoughts. Instead of seeking and asking God these questions, I would seek my answers in people; especially, the serpents… I mean "men" I dated.

In Genesis chapter three, the serpent could not wait to approach Eve. She was new to earth and fresh flesh for him to work his magic. He began the conversation and, of course, Eve responded. Isn't it funny how we, as women, tend to have Eve's personality? We always

3

have a response or rebuttal to prove we know something, even if we do not have all the information. Anyway, the serpent continues to let Eve talk for the last time in chapter three before he intervened in verse five.

*"For God knows that in the day you eat of it your eyes will be opened, and you will be like God, knowing the difference between good and evil and blessing and calamity."* **Gen 3:5 Amp**

When we are far from God, we are free game for the enemy. Most of the time, if not all of the time, he uses our five senses against us (hearing, seeing, touching, tasting, and smelling) because our sixth sense (The Holy Spirit) is inactive. This is how I ended up in a relationship that caused disruption in my life. Bae was a great person, but the enemy will use our dysfunction to cause corruption in our life, which leads us into sin. The enemy set up the scene really good by saying what I wanted to hear and, of course, making Bae attractive in my eyes. Have you fallen into a trap like this, or was it just me? I was sold on the temptation just like Eve was in verse six.

*"And when the woman **saw** that the tree was good (suitable and pleasant) for food and that it was delightful to look at, and a tree to be desired in order to make one wise, she **took** of its fruit and **ate**; and she gave some also to her husband, and he ate."* **Gen 3:6 Amp**

Eve went against everything she knew she was not supposed to do. She disregarded the red flags and became vulnerable because she thought she was going to gain something she lacked—knowledge about herself. Maybe you have never been tempted to taste the forbidden fruit in a relationship, but maybe you ate something you were not supposed to eat, or you took something that did not belong to you. Either way you went against what God, your parents, or your friends told you not to do. I don't know about you, but I have those friends who will tell me "GIRL, DON'T DO IT!" So, let me tell you... GIRL, DON'T DO IT; IT'S NOT WORTH IT!

I was so deep in the relationship the good was turning into evil, and my blessings were turning into calamity. We were so hungry sometimes, literally, we were willing to do anything. I ate the fruit and gave some to Bae, so he could eat too. Our relationship went from the garden to the wilderness quickly that year, but of course I was silent. I could not tell my family the turmoil I was in. The only thing that was keeping us together was our brokenness and sex. Our brokenness completed the puzzle, and the sex created a baby.

In 2006 the turn-up was real. Shortly after my birthday, I found out I was pregnant. I was scared of what my family would say because I was still in college on a track scholarship, but I eventually told my mom. She was furious because Bae could barely take care of his first child, and he dropped out of school. I would be angry too, but you could not tell me anything. I stood up for him... in my mama's house. I was definitely crazy in love by then.

Weeks had passed by, and I was scheduled to go for my 12-week checkup the following Monday, but on Sunday night, as I was lying in bed, my water broke. I didn't even know I was in labor. I ran to the bathroom, and as soon as I sat down on the toilet blood was gushing out. I called my sister and mom into the bathroom, and we drove straight to the ER clinic. I was very scared and numb about the situation.

We arrived at the clinic, and I was immediately sent back to a room. Things were happening so fast, and Bae's car was broken, so he could not meet us at the clinic. The doctor cleaned out my pelvic area and put parts of my baby in a urine cup. When I looked at the cup, I felt like another piece of me was taken... another part of me I was unable to know... I called Bae and told him we lost the baby, and that's when we fell apart. We were both crying our eyes out.

The doctor came back in and said I would have to go to the hospital because they were not able to remove the entire baby. We drove to the hospital, and they were able to remove the rest of the sac. The doctor was also able to determine the sex of the baby because I was further along than I thought. God had better plans for our son. He is definitely in a better place because his young parents were not ready to raise a child of God.

After losing our son, I was dealing with depression because I was holding everything in. Bae was dealing with his own emotions, but he was right there consoling me. At one point he had to stop me and tell me to let everything I was holding on to out. Later that month he told me that he was moving back home to Fort Worth. *Umm... so now I'm losing you, too?*! I had made him the center of my life. He was my everything.

After he moved back home, I was there every payday weekend. We planned to get married, and I was going to move there with him. Once school started back, I was unable to go to Fort Worth every other weekend. During this time a lot of insecurities began to grow in our relationship because we were so used to being with each other all day, every day. We both had good reason to be insecure because the one thing that was keeping us together could no longer be the glue. We said we were engaged, yet we would date other people. Even though we were honest with one another about what we were doing, it still broke our trust. We were chained to each other, but the chain allowed us the option to connect with other people.

Our relationship was spiraling out of control, and the tattoo of our names on my ankle became less significant. I turned it into a dying rose that represented our son and our relationship. We tried on several occasions to make it work, but we were growing apart. The forbidden fruit that once satisfied my taste buds was no longer, and the aroma of the fruit made me sick to my stomach. I will always love Bae, but he could no longer be my god.

I turned around to God and realized He was standing there the entire time. My heart's desire was to seek Him and ask for forgiveness. I needed to know who I was. I blocked out the voice of the enemy, and put my blinders on so I could only see and hear from Him. If you can relate to my story, I am here to tell you, "JUST TURN AROUND." You may feel lost in the wilderness, but God is there. He is with you! He still loves you and, most of all, He forgives you for the choices you have made. Now, just forgive yourself. Surrender your life to Christ; He will see you through.

After having my "Ah Hah" moment of turning around to face God, I started walking with Him. I was attending the church my ex-boyfriend invited me to back in 2004. I know what you are probably thinking. *Out of all the churches in Houston, you chose the one your ex goes to?* He wasn't happy about it either, but I really loved this church, so I joined the summer of 2007. Nobody was going to stop me from being in a place I was called to be. I was focused on getting my life all the way together, so I didn't need any distractions. Once I declared "No Distractions," every distraction possible started coming my way.

At the time I was still working for the same organization, but this year there were more students from my university working there. Even though I kept to myself, my eyes were doing something else. There was plenty of eye candy, but I decided to keep things professional. Plus, I didn't want to repeat the same cycle. The summer passed, and the fall semester was coming to an end when I bumped into one of the guys I worked with during the summer. We exchanged a few words, and later that night we connected through Facebook. We later exchanged numbers and went on our first date. I was so excited to finally connect with another guy other than Bae.

We shared a chemistry and connection I never experienced before. I thought I was falling in love all over again. During this stage of my life, I confused chemistry and connection with love. I have learned that you can have chemistry with a stranger, and you can connect with a person through pain. Pain was the glue that kept us together. We were both coming out of toxic relationships hoping this one would be different. A few weeks went by, and I found myself spending all of my free time with him. We would meet up during his lunch break, and then hang out after his shift was over. I was unconsciously repeating the same cycle.

One day I arrived a few minutes before it was time for him to get off work, so I waited for him in the car. When it was time for him to get off, he walked out with another girl. From their interaction you could tell they were more than friends. He hugged her and came over to my car like nothing had just happened. With an attitude I asked, "Who was that?" He said, "She is just a friend from high school. She brought me the new J's from her store." I nonchalantly said, "Okay." I let it go because I wanted to show him that I trusted him and was not insecure, even though that moment caused me to feel less than.

A month had passed, and we were on our way to my friend's wedding. When we arrived at the reception, he kept looking around paranoid. After we found our seats, I went to the buffet to make a plate, and as soon as I sat down a girl approached our table and said, "Baby, do you need me to make you a plate?" I looked at her like *No, she didn't,* and then I looked at him with rage and disbelief. He quickly said, "No, I'm good." As she walked away, I realized she was the same girl he'd hugged at his job. I was so angry we ended up leaving the reception early. I felt very betrayed because I'd trusted him.

I ignored the red flag, and we continued to date. During this time we argued a lot, and my self-esteem was dwindling. I know you are probably saying, "That couldn't have been me!" or "I wouldn't put up with that!" We all say things we wouldn't or couldn't do until we are in a situation we don't know how to get out of. God continued to reveal his character to me, but I was too blind to see it—until one day I called him to meet up for lunch and, to my surprise, he was at Hooters having a "business meeting". Really... a business meeting—at Hooters? Of course I did not believe him, so I drove to Hooters in my sister's car and waited for him to come out.

An hour later, I heard his loud laugh in the parking lot. When I looked up, he was holding hands and kissing another girl. So many thoughts were going through my mind, as tears began to run down my face. *Should I run him over with the car? Should I confront them in the parking lot? What should I do?* I drove away angry and hurt. After I stopped crying, I called him screaming, "It's over! I'm done with you!" By the time I parked the car in the driveway, he was pulling up behind me. When he got out the car, he starting to apologize and ask for forgiveness. I accepted his apology, and I told him we could no longer be together. We broke up, but we would still keep in touch.

I had one more semester before graduating, and things became more stressful. I would run back to my comfort zone and call him so we could hang out because "I missed him". One night I missed him a little too much, and I was right back where we started. Almost five weeks had passed, and my menstrual cycle went missing. I blamed it on stress because it had been inconsistent lately. I talked to him about my cycle not coming on time, and he suggested I take a pregnancy test. After school I went straight home to take it and before I knew it I was standing in the bathroom holding a positive pregnancy test in my hand. I looked in the mirror feeling lost, disappointed, and just plain stupid! *How did I let this happen... again*? I asked myself. I took a picture of it and sent it to my friend to get a second opinion because I could not be pregnant right now and not by him.

Our relationship was rocky, and I did not want to bring a child into our chaos. My friend confirmed that I was definitely pregnant. I called and told him the news and to my surprise he was overly excited about having a baby. I was thinking, *It is easy for you to be excited because you aren't the one carrying a baby out of wedlock. We are not even boyfriend/girlfriend, and how am I going to tell my parents?* I scheduled an ultrasound appointment to find out how far along I was in my pregnancy because I had to have all the facts and plans in order before presenting this to my mama. Even with all the facts and plans she was disappointed in me for the second time.

I knew Mom wanted the best for me, and being a single mother was not one of them. I watched her make ends meet and comfort me when my dad didn't keep his promises. These were just the things I was aware of while growing up. Before graduation I was offered a job, which made my parents feel a little more at ease. Toward the end of my second trimester things were going well. Our baby girl was healthy, and our relationship was thriving like never before. I knew we were going to be together for the rest of our lives. Little did I know, this ideal would not become my reality.

On a Saturday night he asked me to pay his phone bill online (with his credit card) because he did not have access to the internet at the time. I paid the bill, and I also paid close attention to his call records. There were three numbers that showed up consistently. One of the numbers were mine, and the other two began with different area codes. I turned into the FBI, and found out the girls' name, where they were from, where they currently live, and how they looked just in case we crossed paths. Our paths eventually crossed at his home church. I was sitting next to his mom while he went to help set up chairs. When he was walking back to sit down, he spoke to her, "Hey, Chi Town!" like there was nothing going on between the two of them. She was sitting right behind us... in church! After church, 'Chi Town' was blowing his phone up. He finally called her back while I was inside the house resting. I could hear him yelling at her like she was in the wrong. The reverse psychology worked because she continued to talk to him according to the call records. Yes, I checked the records frequently.

I decided to hold all of this information in until after my daughter was born because I did not want to go into premature labor. Well, that plan did not go as planned because my daughter was ready to come in time for Thanksgiving, but my doctor was able to stop the contractions. I stayed in the hospital for an entire week and was later released on bed rest for the duration of my pregnancy. While I was on bed rest he would come visit for an hour and leave to go do "who knows what with you know who". At this point I was numb to the disrespect, and I was ready for this pregnancy to be over.

I was 38 weeks, and my doctor took me off the medication that was stopping my contractions. The night before my water broke, I told him to stay by the phone because I knew I was going to go into labor. I stayed up talking and joking with my sister until two in the morning. An hour later my water broke, and while heading to the hospital I was calling his phone, but there was no answer. I called his mom and she arrived at the hospital before he did. That scenario did not add up because I thought he was at home. My contractions became stronger, and the words out of my mouth were uncontrollable. I was frustrated with him and the contractions. Eventually, I asked for an epidural and a few hours later my world changed.

My daughter knocked some sense into my head, and I saw my life differently from that moment on. During my twelve-week maternity leave, we both agreed he would take care our daughter during the day while I went back to work because we were trying to avoid daycare costs. While getting ready for work one morning, I received a phone call from his mother informing me that he was in jail. I could not dwell in my frustration because I had to find someone to keep my daughter at the last minute or call into work. This was my first dose of reality of what it means to be a single mother. I was able to drop off my daughter at my grandmother's house and head to work.

My bottled up frustration eventually exploded once he returned home from jail. I finally confronted him about the call records and 'Chi Town'. I refused to be hooked on his mental, emotional, and physical retractable leash. It was time for me to take the leash off rather than wait for him to change his mind about wanting to commit to me. I deserved better, and my daughter deserved a better mother. Begging on his knees did not stop me from cutting all ties from him that night. As I walked away with my daughter, I did not know I was walking into a life that would challenge me as a woman and a mother on another level.

Shortly after our official breakup, he went back to jail for a longer sentence. Those months felt like eternity. I enrolled my daughter into an extended hour daycare, and my mother would pick her up at night because I started working the second shift to make enough money to pay for her expenses. I felt like I was on a merry-go-round. I had some good and some bad days, as my life continued to go around and around. I felt as though I was not making any progress because I was just trying to survive the setbacks. At this point I was feeling overwhelmed, and I just needed a BREAK! This was the longest I had been single, or should I say "felt lonely" in years.

My loneliness led me to Match.com. There were so many guys

who were compatible, but only one caught my attention. We had a lot in common, and I could not wait to meet him in person. The day finally came for us to go on our date. I was very excited because:

1. I was getting out the house by myself.

2. I was going to have an adult conversation.

3. I was going to meet a man.

Can you say I was winning? Or, so I thought. While I was on my way to the restaurant, I received a call from him saying that he would not be able to make it because somebody egged his car. *Really?!?! How old are we again?* I thought to myself. I politely said, "Ok, we can just reschedule for another time." Why did I say that? I was definitely turned off, but I ignored the red flag… AGAIN!

I wanted to feel wanted, and during this time I was willing to sacrifice myself to gain affection from a stranger. I wanted to show him that I was understanding, and that I was worth committing to. We eventually went out on a few dates, and he told me that he THOUGHT he'd found his match. My gullible-self believed him, and I logged onto Match.com to cancel my subscription because I thought I had found the one. As soon as I cancelled my subscription his fear of commitment accused me of spending time with my child's father. I removed my shame, and I was forced to tell him the truth. I told him that I don't have a lot of free time because my child's father is in jail, so I am doing everything by myself.

He said that he understood my situation, and we could make time based on my availability. I was relieved to hear that because I did not want to lose him. I would make an effort by trying to see him once a week, but he began acting distant. Luckily, my daughter's father was released from jail around this time, and I was able to go on more dates. However, something in my gut told me to check Match.com, and when I searched for his name, his profile was still active. I felt so stupid. I could not believe I was getting played... again! I refused to ignore another red flag. I ended the relationship and stopped to take a look at myself in the mirror.

I ignored the red flags because I desired a covenant with men whom I thought loved me. Little did I know that I was also ignoring a true covenant with a man who died for me. Jesus sacrificed his life for me and loved me enough to shed His blood for me. The guys I dated sacrificed me, and I allowed it to happen. My brokenness chose those relationships. Fear of rejection made me love them more than I loved myself. Fear of loneliness made me settle for less than I deserved. I cannot expect another person to finish the work I started.

No human can complete me; only God can. I cannot punish a person for the pain that the previous person caused me, and if you are experiencing the same pain from a new person you must examine yourself. You are the common denominator! Why do you continue to function in dysfunction? As a single mother, I had to stop and ask myself this question because I saw my daughter watching my every move. I did not want to raise another broken daughter who has the potential to become a broken and bitter woman.

I made up in my mind that I had to break the generational brokenness that was carried down from the single mothers in my family. I put in the work that required me to face my fears and insecurities. When I addressed the root of the problem the fruit of bitterness, anger, jealousy, and envy stopped growing. People attracted to this type of fruit stopped picking me to be around. I know the process is not easy, but looking into my daughter's eyes kept me encouraged. I refused to let her, and most of all God, down. My desires changed, and I respected myself enough to keep boundaries in place.

I have been on dates but none of them have led to a relationship, or even a second date. I am whole enough to recognize whether a person has my best interest for me and my daughter. I used to confuse chemistry and connection with love. Just know that you can have chemistry with many people, and you can sometimes connect with others through pain. I know sometimes you just want someone to rescue you from this thing called life and single motherhood. Just know that every breath you take is God confirming His presence. Being a single mother can be challenging, and trying to co-parent (if you have that option) is a tug of war.

All of this can be overwhelming, but I am learning that all God wants me to do is surrender so that he can rightfully take His position as my friend, father, and husband. He is the opposite of the worldly man because He waits until you give Him permission to move. He is not an initiator. He does not take over your life until He gets an invite from you. Are you ready to surrender? Are you ready to wave your white flag? Before you answer those questions, let us talk about what it looks like to surrender. I had given my life to Christ years ago, but I was not living as though Christ was in my life. I knew what was required of me, and for that reason I was afraid to fully commit at that time because I did not want to leave familiar. Like many women, I became comfortable in uncomfortable situations and immune to functioning in dysfunction.

I had a rhythm or routine that I was not ready to walk away from, even though it was causing me pain, low self-esteem, self-destruction, anxiety, and depression. I can remember going to the doctor because I was having heart palpitations and an irregular heartbeat, but the doctor could not find anything wrong. I eventually faced the facts and knew that it was my toxic relationship causing my health to suffer. Right then and there I had to make a decision—Do I want to suffer or surrender? I loved myself enough to surrender. I made a conscious decision to live for God and not for selfish desires. I was finally ready to address what was going on inside of me. I asked God, "Why was I wanting to be in a relationship so badly? To feel loved? What is love?" He led me to a scripture I have read many times, but this time it was different.

1 Corinthians 13: 4-8 (AMP), "Love endures with patience and serenity, love is kind and thoughtful, and is not jealous or envious; love does not brag and is not proud or arrogant. It is not rude; it is not self-seeking, it is not provoked [nor overly sensitive and easily angered]; it does not take into account a wrong endured. It does not rejoice at injustice but rejoices with the truth [when right and truth prevail]. Love bears all things [regardless of what comes], believes all things [looking for the best in each one], hopes all things [remaining steadfast during difficult times], endures all things [without weakening]. Love never fails [it never fades nor ends]. But as for prophecies, they will pass away; as for tongues, they will cease; as for the gift of special knowledge, it will pass away."

After reading this I knew I had a lot of work to do. I had never loved a man like this, and a man has never shown me this type of love. What I was seeking from a boyfriend at the time was something only God could give me. The first step in surrendering is admitting your wrongs. I asked God to forgive me for the broken decisions I made in my past. I went all the way back to childhood because I was determined to be delivered from coping with dysfunction. I wanted to be healed. I told Him my innermost secrets. Part of surrendering is becoming transparent with yourself and God. Being transparent is for you. You will feel naked and vulnerable before God, but trust that He will cover you. I had to trust that He would acknowledge my vulnerability and not take advantage of it like men did in past relationships. When I became naked before God, only then was I able to fully appreciate His unconditional love.

He will begin to shape and mold you into the original thought He had about you before you were in your mother's womb. The transformation will not be easy. There will be moments when you want to give up because growing up can be painful, but you have to believe you've been equipped with the capacity to endure or to remain steadfast during difficult times. Remember that He will show His love, so that you can mimic His love toward yourself and others. Surrendering also means you must let go of old behavior.

I know this is a lot to take in when you have not implemented this behavior on a consistent basis. Trust me! My child's father has challenged me in ALL areas. During this process I had to make up in mind that I would not give into my old nature.

Galatians 5: 19-20 (AMP), "Now the practices of the sinful nature are clearly evident: they are sexual immorality, impurity, sensuality (total irresponsibility, lack of self-control), idolatry, sorcery, hostility, strife, jealousy, fits of anger, disputes, dissensions, factions [that promote heresies], envy, drunkenness, riotous behavior, and other things like these."

Giving up these things are not a walk in the park. It requires recommitting on a daily basis—sometimes every hour. I had to learn how to guard my mind, body, and spirit if I wanted to make this change permanent and not temporary. What does guarding my mind, body, and spirit look like? I have to be mindful that what goes in will eventually come out.

**My Mind:** The mind is consumed with thoughts, but those thoughts are triggered by the five senses (eyes, ears, nose, mouth, and hands). I have to be careful of what I watch, listen to, smell, taste, and touch. What you watch and listen to can be a distraction that leads to destruction. It can easily plant seeds that can lead to the sinful nature I previously mentioned. Now, I know you might be wondering how can what you smell, taste, and touch lead you to letting your guard down? Well, those three senses can affect the body.

**My Body:** Have you ever smelled, tasted, or touched something that triggered a behavior? Of course you have! Let's talk about food. Food was connected to my emotions. My emotional instability led me to eat excessively, or not at all. My body was suffering because of it. I would become fatigued, vitamin deficient, and my weight would fluctuate. My emotions not only led me to horrible eating habits, but sexual immorality. My fear of loneliness and the need to feel "loved" was associated with sex. I had to tell myself that I would not be ruled by my emotions. God was leading me, and He gave me authority to take control of my body. My mind and body impacted my spirit.

**My Spirit:** I have learned that my spirit is the most delicate part of me. I have to be careful not to allow any and everybody into my life because their spirit can affect my spirit. Some women fail to realize that who we become intimate with matters. It does not always have to be a sexual relationship, it can be an emotional one. The person does not have to be a mate, it can be a platonic friendship male or female. Be careful when you find yourself letting your guard down and allowing unqualified people to enter your secret place. I had given people a key to my place they could not afford to maintain. I had sexual and emotional soul ties to men that were broken little boys. I thought that we could help each other become whole, but our broken pieces pierced each other's scabs and made new wombs. I thought that ending the relationship would heal me from my brokenness, but it only left me more broken.

In one of my relationships I experienced the stages of mourning:

1. Denial – I did not want to believe he would let me end the relationship. I just knew he would fight for us. Of course he didn't, so it led to #2.
2. Anger – I was so mad and over it. I blocked him out of my life.
3. Bargaining – Sometimes, I would go back and forth about unblocking him. What if he was trying to contact me to resurrect what I killed?
4. Depression – The slightest contact awakened the little piece of hope I needed to let go of. I found myself fighting

depression and trying to move forward again.

5.   Acceptance – I finally accepted that things are never going to work between us. What I killed was dead, and I couldn't hold on to something that was not there.

I had to heal from self-inflicting wombs and recover from the damage that person caused me. So, now when I meet a person, I have to discern whether or not they exude the fruit of the spirit or possess a sinful nature. I need people who are going to have a positive influence in my life, and I will do whatever it takes to keep the right people in and the wrong people out. Who are you allowing to enter in to your life?

When I started my journey from suffering to surrendering, I was able to discern a person's motives and intentions rather quickly. I want to walk you through the process I had to put in place to stop ignoring red flags:

(<sup>I</sup>)   **Don't ignore the facts because you desire the fairytale more.**

The FIRST thing I had to do was stop ignoring the facts. My mom and grandmother would always tell me, "When people show you who they are, believe them." I ignored all the signs because I was waiting for him to reach his potential. I heard him say many things that would be a deal breaker for me, but I chose to not listen to the truth that was coming out of his mouth. I wanted the fairytale story more than I wanted God. Girl, if he tells you the truth the first time do not wait until the 99<sup>th</sup> time to believe him. Do not ignore the temper tantrums, abusive language, demeaning comments, excessive cheating, etc. All of this is not worth you risking your mind, body, and spirit for the fairytale from hell.

21

## ⏻ Red means Stop, not Go!

When you are first taught how to drive, you learn that you go on a green light, but you must come to a complete stop at a red light. If you keep driving through the red light, there is a great possibility you will be involved in an accident—an accident that could have been prevented if you would have stopped at the red light. Many of us get into a relationship risking our lives by moving forward in the relationship when we need to end it. All women have an intuition or that gut feeling, but I call it the Holy Spirit. Have you ever done something and afterwards you find yourself saying, "Something told me not to do that?" Yes? Okay, that is the Holy Spirit. The Holy Spirit gives you instruction before corruption. I knew not to start the relationship, but I ignored the red light and sacrificed my life in hopes that my insurance (I mean God) would cover it.

## ⏻ A good man vs. A godly man

Lastly, I had to know what I wanted. When I would date guys, I was trying to figure out what I wanted. I was Dora the Explorer! As I began building my relationship with God, He began to show me what a husband looks like. I just wanted a good man, and that is what I attracted. Aside from our brokenness we had a connection and chemistry, but we lacked a Godly/spiritual connection. The guys I would date were led by their flesh rather than led by the Spirit. Our flesh is inconsistent, and we are more prone to make decisions based on how we feel. The human heart is deceitful and wicked, that is why we have the Holy Spirit to guide us in the right direction. When a man is led by God, he will not influence you to go against Him. When I go on a date, I am looking for a man with a plan. A plan that includes a purpose that leads to prosperity. Prosperity for the kingdom of God and his family.

You need to know where a man is going before following his lead because you do not want to end up wandering in the wilderness. This advice applies to you as well. If you do not have a plan that includes purpose, how will you know if you two are equally yoked? Take your time to get to know yourself before rushing to date or to marry someone. Do not place expectations on another person when you are having a hard to meeting them yourself.

I pray that this chapter has helped you on your journey as a single mother, revealed areas that need improvement, or confirmed that you are headed on the right path. I want you to know that you are not walking alone. We are here with you in spirit, and remember God is always present. Always remember to pray, be patient, and persevere during this season. You've got this!

## Meet Sylvia Phillips

**Where do you find your POWER?**

I find POWER in my relationship with God. When I find myself losing energy, becoming afraid or discouraged, I am always reminded of who I am and whose I am, and that restores my POWER. I also find POWER with the unconditional love of my family.

# CHAPTER 2

## BEING SINGLE IS NOT A DEATH THREAT

### Single Life after a Divorce

#### By Sylvia Phillips

———————◆———————

In many cases, for a woman, the pinnacle of adulthood and achieving the "good life" is entering into a marriage. This union shapes much of a woman's validation as a successful person and path to motherhood. The phrase "for better or for worse" is more than an overused cliché. Certainly, I have experienced the highs and lows of entering into holy matrimony. After two failed marriages and being a single mother, I am compelled to share with you stories of my struggles and triumphs during and after my divorces. The following memoirs are provided to you as words of encouragement and to present you with thought provoking questions to assist you on your journey as a single mother. I pray that my story invigorates you with confidence and love. More importantly, after reading this chapter you will be empowered to be the woman, mother, friend, lover, and the individual God has called you to be.

The American Psychological Association quotes the

Encyclopedia of Psychology as indicating that 40 to 50 percent of marriages in the United States will end in divorce. The end of a marriage can be a traumatic experience for everyone involved in the relationship. In fact, a divorce can feel similar to losing a loved one; however, be encouraged because living single is not a death sentence. The single life can actually usher you into a renewed life of purpose, especially after enduring a comatose marriage. Individuals who have experienced a divorce know that often there is a grieving period. During this period not only will you grieve, you are also forced to learn to date, care and counsel children, and solely manage finances. Personally, I have experienced the joys of marriage, grief of divorce, and the refreshing feeling of being single multiple of times. Ultimately, happiness comes once you learn to deal with and overcome the grief associated with your divorce.

According to B.L.J. Burke, there are seven stages of grief during and after a divorce: denial, pain, fear, anger, bargaining, guilt, depression, and acceptance. Wow! Those are a lot of emotions to experience just to be happy after a divorce! Yes, your feelings will be everywhere when you leave a marriage, but the joy you gain once you rediscover who you are is priceless.

For instance, in many cases, denial sets you up to believe that this can't happen to you. Guess, what? It can and it did... you are now *single*. During and after my first divorce was final, I remained in a constant state of denial for years. Before the failed marriage, the man I thought was my first love had already abandoned me at the altar. So, my self-assurance regarding love and marriage was a little lacking. Even though I was timid about planning and saying I was getting married, I was young and thought that in order to be complete I needed to be married. I was afraid of being single. Reflecting back on my thinking at that time, I realized my frame of mind was immature and juvenile. Well, as immature as it was, we ran to the courthouse, were married by the Justice of the Peace, and had a few blissful years. No one told me that once the thrill was gone, the marriage would be over, and I would be single. The day I left the marriage, I thought my life was over. I was embarrassed, angry, and hurt. At this critical juncture what I didn't realize was that my life was just beginning.

During my grieving period, I experienced every emotion imaginable. Initially, I was afraid that if I were kind, I would definitely be taken advantage of again. So, I built a wall of security and self-pity. My anger was so intense, I took my situation out on everyone around me. Friends and family stopped calling me because all I did was unconsciously complain about how bad I had it. The only thoughts that occupied my mind was that I am single, no one loves me; I'm a single parent, and I have to do everything on my own. Now, I fully understand that when I isolated myself behind my "secure" wall, I was setting myself up to be alone and afraid. Conversely, it wasn't a wall that kept people out; it was a wall that kept me in quarantine from those who loved me.

The isolation that I withstood was a time of rediscovery for me. I spent a lot of time with God reading, listening to His direction, and journaling. Not only did I read the bible, but I also read books that facilitated laughter, such as *Me Talk Funny* by David Sedaris. The laughter helped me to understand that no matter what we are going through, life must go on. I had a daughter, and she needed me. I learned that happiness is a choice. I could have chosen to remain isolated, angry and hurt, but I chose happiness—not only for me, but also for my daughter. However, freeing yourself from the agonizing bondage of a failed marriage can be a daunting task. You have to first admit that you are grieving over a marriage you were committed to no matter how bad it was. In all actuality, it's hard to see yourself single when you vowed to love a person for the remainder of your life. Ultimately, acknowledgement is the first step to acceptance. In the final analysis you can't accept that you are single until you have acknowledged that the marriage is over.

Once you begin to accept that your marriage is over and you are single, you resolve that single life is not so bad. Those who choose a Christian-oriented, spiritual path, begin to live life according to God's plans. You are no longer angry or afraid, for you are comforted by the reality that God is with you. From time-to-time you may feel a little concerned about being single because you really don't fully understand that being single doesn't make you a statistic, but it allows you to elevate without disruption. One may ask what does this mean? Well, it means that during your marriage you were focused on your husband and children. You set aside your dreams and encouraged your spouse to pursue his aspirations. First, it means you can now devote your time to you and your child/children. It means you can move from the pity-party and begin to thrive. Second, it means you can start the business you always wanted or continue your education. Third, it means you are the sole decision-maker in your life, and the only other person you need to consult is God. Finally, Ii means you are free to start a new and revitalized life being single!

At this point, the divorce is over, and you have overcome your grief. You have a solid prayer life and consistent relationship with God; you've gone to counseling, you journal on your feelings, and say daily affirmations. Everyone begins to tell you it's time to start dating. Maybe you're not ready for a steady relationship, but you agree that it's time to step out and enjoy life. It is important to be positive and optimistic about the possibility of entering a healthy relationship.

Oftentimes after a divorce we must shift our way of thinking. In my case, I needed to remind myself that there are really no fairy tale marriages. It is a myth that the prince comes and kisses the princess, and they live life happily ever after. If you are truly healed, you will not charge each new relationship with the previous relationships' bills. Your new prospective mate is not responsible for your past hurts and disappointments. Remember, you are single and have the POWER to choose what makes you happy.

In the final analysis, the problem I had after my first marriage was over was that I wasn't truly healed. I was a creature of habit, and I chose the same type of men. I loved a sweet-talker, and they knew it from the onset. In addition, my low self-esteem kept me in a place that made me believe I needed a man to tell me I was pretty, smart, and sexy. Like most new relationships, I was treated like that princess, which we know doesn't exist. However, after a few months those accolades ceased to exist. In the process I began to feel insecure and question his every move. Inevitably, I fell in love knowing he didn't feel the same about me as I felt about him. He told me upfront that he was not looking for a serious relationship, but because he was attempting to woo me and periodically gave me his attention, I believed he did. Notwithstanding the fact that I was receiving this attention under false pretenses, I did what felt best and went with the flow. In the end, I learned that one must heal before you have that first date. Please make healing a priority!

Another huge concern for many single mothers after divorce is finances. It doesn't matter how much money you make or do not make, when you are accustomed to two incomes and now you have one, that's a concern. Maybe you were the only one working in the relationship; well, your concern is what to do with all this extra money you will be keeping now. But, that's probably not the case with many women. You probably combined your funds to pay bills, or you had your bills and he had his bills, and then there were the household bills.

Whatever you did financially while you were married will change. As a single divorcee, you will need new strategies for saving money, creating a budget, have financial discipline, and knowing your numbers.

## ⏻ Savings

Saving small amounts of money early on is a sure way to increase your finances. If you don't already have a savings account, run to your bank and open one. Most banks will allow you to open a savings account for as little as twenty-five dollars. If you are working, have money automatically put into the account every paycheck. Every year after you receive a raise, increase the amount of money going to your savings. Many of you may not have money right away. That's okay; here is what you do. Every time you buy something at the store and you receive change, put that change away in a jar until you have enough to open your account. Remember, you have to be creative.

Another thing, I did for my finances was to make contributions to an IRA account. I had no idea about these benefits because I was uneducated when it came to my finances. But, I soon realized that saving and contributing to the IRA helped me save a year's salary.

Not every divorced single woman will be able to save her annual pay; nevertheless, she can save enough for emergencies.

## ⏻ Create a Budget

As a divorced single mother, I quickly realized that I wouldn't survive without a budget. I didn't understand the budgeting process, but I knew that if I was to make it from paycheck to paycheck, I needed a plan. I learned that if I wanted to get out of financial distress, I would need to take baby steps and not compare myself to others. I needed a budget! First, I listed out any money I had coming in on a monthly basis; however, I didn't include child support because I wasn't sure if that would be constant. Secondly, I wrote out all my bills and monies going out monthly. Don't forget to budget the money you will be putting into your savings every paycheck. Finally, for one month, I carried a tablet and I intentionally wrote out every penny I spent. This helped me learn that there were things I was used to in my marriage that I didn't need, nor did I really want. I carefully selected how I spent money.

## ⏻ Discipline

Discipline is a learned behavior. It is also the key to maintaining your finances. For many years I was doing financially what my single friends were doing. Spending money without saving or a budget. After my divorce, I realized that many of my single friends had nice cars and were living comfortably. Needless to say, they had not yet married and didn't have children. Ultimately, I had to focus and do what was best for me and my daughter.

Sometimes my friends could not understand when I said no to

shopping and happy hour. If you are choosing to be disciplined in your finances you must shift your wants to needs. You can't spend money on trendy bags and expensive shoes. If you just feel you need to buy something, there are many resale shops that carry out of season items that are just as nice as the in-season items. In fact, I shopped at second hands stores for my daughter and myself for the first couple of years after my divorce. Only purchase what you can truly afford. Discipline is saving your money until you can pay cash. I learned that it was more beneficial to watch my savings account grow rather than fill my closet with items I may use only three or four times.(2) teach you how to invest without your spouse; (3) assist you with understanding your financial goals as opposed to your financial needs; and (4) help you with complicated taxes.

It was during my single life that I learned the importance of investing my money wisely. However, I had to understand my numbers and how much I could invest. One of my biggest fears was that I didn't have enough to invest. I was surprised to learn that I could begin with as little as one thousand dollars. After a few visits with the investment banker, I bought the books *Investing for Dummies* and *Understanding the Stock Market*. These books were the best investments I could have made.

Not only did I wait for material items, I began cooking at home. As single parents we are quick to go to the fast food drive-through for dinner. Cooking at home afforded me the opportunity to have leftovers for lunch. Not only did this help my finances, but it also helped me eat healthier. Single life did not mean I had to be broke, but I did need to have discipline in every area of my life.

## ⏻ Understand Your Financial Situation

As women we are private creatures. We don't like talking with others about how much money we have or don't have. Sometimes we may not have the financial education to grasp our numbers. Speaking with a financial or investing individual soon after divorce can help ease some of your fears about money. This may be someone in your bank, or someone who was referred. I know you may feel as though you don't have much after the divorce, but you probably have more than you think. The banker can help you in several ways. For instance, he/she can: (1) decide whether or not you should consolidate all the accounts you had while you were married, so you don't have to pay so many fees.

Also, don't be afraid to know your credit score. After divorcing your score may drop considerably. But, you can get a free credit report once a year from one or all of the major credit reporting agencies such as: Experian, TransUnion, and Equifax. If you are not satisfied with your numbers or feel there are things on your report that should not be there, you can write them and, most of the time, things can be removed. It is imperative that you fight for financial freedom.

Once you have read and understood your credit report, now it is time to start contacting your credit card companies and utility companies to lower your rates. If you were in good standing with these companies and fell behind because of the divorce, have an open and honest communication with the companies. Ask them to give you a second chance, and many of the companies will grant your request.

⏻ **Purge**

A good way to make money to open that savings account you read about earlier is to get rid of things you really don't need. Maybe you downsized to a smaller house or an apartment. Have a garage sale, or even take items to a consignment store. If you don't like the idea of a garage sale, you could have an estate sale and make the buyers set an appointment, so you don't have so many people in the house at one time.

Another way to purge would be to sell those books you have been meaning to trash. Half price bookstores are always looking for books. What about those cell phones lying around? Every dime helps with your savings account, so why not take the phones and get cash? In fact, you should do an inventory of your home to see what can be purged and turned into cash.

As long as you are trying, God will place people and things in your life to help you in your journey as a single woman after divorce. Don't be afraid to ask for help or to ask questions about things you don't understand. You are not ignorant if you don't know… only if you don't ask, knowing you don't know.

A few things to remember about finances after divorce: the key to saving is discipline in every aspect of your spending; if you can't pay cash for it, don't buy it; save even if it is $10.00 a paycheck; and talk to an investment banker to help map out a budget for investing. You have the POWER to be financially savvy.

Not only does a single woman have to manage her finances, she must also find a way to take care of her children. She sometimes has to take the father's role, meet with schools, counsel or meet with counselors, attend extracurricular activities, prepare meals, clean house, do laundry, etc.—the list could go on and on. Ladies, you really don't have to do it alone. Your children did not divorce their father. Try to remain friendly with your spouse. Notice I did not say to remain friends because there is a difference between friendly and friends.

For instance, friendly only means you should be nice to an individual; whereas, a friend is a good listener, responds quickly, an encourager, is loyal, is a friend unconditionally, and does not expect personal gain. Being friendly should suffice. Don't use your children to get back at their father because it is not fair to them, and it may even backfire.

An older cousin, Mrs. Myrtle, taught me something very valuable when it came to the relationship of my daughter and her father. Over 30 years ago, she told me that my daughter wasn't a piece of property that I could rent out to her father twice a month. This was so powerful that it still resonates with me today. I had to understand that whether I received child support or not, her father was still her father, and I had no right to keep her from having a relationship with him. Just as boys need their mothers, girls need their fathers.

As difficult as it may be, **do not** talk negative about your child's father in a space that the child can hear. Sometimes we as single women like to talk to our friends about how badly we have been treated, or the lack of money. It will impact your child's relationship with the father even if that is not your intention. Or, sometimes the negative talk might not go as planned, and the child may turn on you.

Remember the child loves both parents equally.

Allow your child to grieve. He or she is grieving the same as you, so allow them to discuss their feelings without judgment. Be honest and open without negativity. Oftentimes, the child believes it may be his/her fault that the parents are divorcing. As a single parent, this is where your counseling will arise. It is extremely important to stress that sometimes people love one another, but cannot live together, and it has nothing to do with the children. Reiterate that both parents love them.

As a single parent, any and everything you do should have you asking yourself how it will affect your child. Sometimes your child may decide that he/she wants to live with their father. If this is the case, and it will not affect the child's safety, don't make him/her feel guilty about the decision they have made. Maybe they want to be near friends or want to attend the same school. Whatever the reason, have a conversation with the child and both parents make a final decision. Children are smart and are good at manipulating one parent over the other. Therefore, have a discussion as if you were co-parenting, so the child understands that no major decisions will be made without the consent of both parents. This gives the child a feeling of unity, which is extremely important. As a single parent you have the POWER to have a healthy child when you maintain a healthy relationship with his/her father.

Just as with anything else in life, being single, happy and having self-worth after divorce is attainable. Assert the following "A's" to your life, and watch your POWER unfold:

> **ACKNOWLEDGE** – It is important to acknowledge that you

are no longer married and must change a few things in your life. Stop calling him for everything.

➤ **ASSESS** – Now that you have acknowledged your marriage is over, begin to assess what needs to be done to regain normalcy in your life. Begin thinking about you.

➤ **ALLOW** – You must allow for flexibility in your life; give yourself time to heal. Remember, you may not be willing, or ready, to do some of the things you did while you were married. You may need to grieve the loss of the relationship.

➤ **ACCEPT** – Ladies, accept that you have the POWER to achieve happiness. Remember happiness is a choice, so choose to be happy.

➤ **ASCEND**– with a Christ-centered lifestyle and frame of mind, believe that you will ascend because the sky's the limit.

Life can change in the twinkling of an eye. If you have never been married and never want to be married, continue to love yourself because that is the best love you can experience. If you have never been married and would like to be married, never give up on love. If you have been married and are recently divorced, know there is life after divorce. Continue to love others and love yourself, no matter where you are as a single parent because being single is not a death sentence.

As you take your journey to healing after divorce, it is important to know who you are, what you want, and what resources are available for success. The following are 10 questions single, divorced mothers should consider:

1. *Why did the relationship end?* This is not a question to cast

blame on either party, but to understand what role you may have played. (i.e. Was I not healed from a previous relationship, did I marry him too soon, did I marry him thinking I could change who he was… so on, and so forth?)

2. ***Prior to becoming a single mom after divorce, what is the single most important thing you wish you would have known?*** As simple as it may sound, you probably would have liked to know that even after divorce you would need to communicate with your partner, especially since children are involved.

3. ***What strengths and skills do you already possess that will make being a single mom less difficult?*** Many women manage their home just as they would a business. Think about what skills you already possess that might be transferable. (i.e. Planning, carpooling, organizing, etc.)

4. ***What steps are you willing to take to involve family and friends in the transition?*** Although inviting everyone to the family barbecue may not be an option, it's a good idea to think about what events may be important to the child(ren) to include others you might otherwise not have included due to the divorce.

5. ***What single parent can I look up to as a mentor, or how can I mentor a single parent?*** You may need someone to help mentor or coach you when you are newly divorced. Sometimes, others can see your strengths a lot better than you can.

6. ***What expectations do you have for your non-single friends?*** Oftentimes, we expect our friends to feel and understand what we are going through even though they are happily married. It severs the friendships because individuals transfer the expectation they had for their husband over to their close friends who, in essence, cannot meet those expectations.

7. ***If you begin dating, what's the best approach for introducing him to your child(ren)?*** Introducing a new individual may be a little difficult, especially if the child(ren) believe Daddy will return. Discussing a new relationship with your child(ren) is imperative. Although you may be ready, your child(ren) may not be, and it is up to you as the parent to make this as comfortable for your child as possible.

8. ***What am I doing for self-care?*** It takes some women longer to begin dating; however, dating is a form of self-care. When taking time away from your child(ren) you often return feeling refreshed and content.

9. ***Who do I have in my village?*** It takes a village to raise a child. Sometimes the father chooses not to be part of the village, but you have others who are more than willing to help when necessary. Don't be afraid to reach out to them.

10. ***How optimistic are you about the future?*** If you don't believe in you, no one else will. What you put into the universe will be what you receive. For example, if you are negative and around negativity, then your life will be full of

statements like: I cannot do it on my own; it will not happen because I am single; I don't have the money because I only have one income; I wish I could do that for my child, but I'm a single mom. On the other hand, if you approach every situation as though you can, then you will.

Divorce does not only raise questions for the adults involved, but the children impacted may also have questions. In most cases, children are resilient and are able to continue life as though nothing happened. But sometimes children want to know what happened, or even if they were the reason for the breakup. Here a few questions children may ask:

1. **What did I do to make Daddy leave?** You may want to reiterate that the child did nothing. It's important for the child to understand that their mommy and daddy still love one another, but in a different way than before; however, the love they have for the child *has not* and *will not* change. Help your child understand that this is a grown-up matter, and he/she need not worry.

2. **Is Daddy coming back home**? If your spouse has no intention of coming home, be honest with the child(ren). If you and your spouse are attempting to work it out, it may not be a good idea to tell them this because you may get their hopes up for something that may not happen.

3. **What will happen to me?** Again, be honest. You can say you will continue to be loved by Mommy and Daddy. If the child is older, you can have a conversation about where he/she would prefer to live. Remember, choosing to live with the father is not an indication that the child doesn't love you.

4. **If Daddy marries someone else and has a child, will that child take my place?** This is probably very scary for the child(ren). You should explain a blended family to your child. Warn them that blended families can be extremely difficult; however, they can also be exciting. Explain to your child that he/she will now have another child to spend time with and even call his or her sibling. But, remind your child that you and his/her father, no matter who enters into the family dynamics, will always love him.

5. **What should I say to my friends?** Remind your child(ren) this was an adult decision. Reassure him/her that they are probably not the only one going through this. If you know of anyone who has gone through a divorce, bring it to the child's attention so that he/she doesn't feel alone. It is important to make this as normal for your child as possible.

Reading has a way of stimulating your brain and engaging your mind. If you are having difficulties processing the idea of divorce, maybe reading can help to relieve some of the pressure, as well as impart knowledge on being single after the divorce. There are books on anything you need—dating, parenting, finances, shifting from married to single, and so much more. Books may not only be beneficial for you, but your child(ren) as well. Reading may be a great catalyst for conveying information regarding divorce to your children in an age appropriate manner. The following are just a few recommendations from my bookshelf that I hope will make it onto your reading list:

1. *POWER Moms: Persevere Overcome Win Empower Restore: Volume 1* by Dr. Sherrie Walton and Co-Authors

2. *12 Months to "A Better You!" The 12 Month Challenge to becoming your best you!* by Dr. Conte Morgan Terrell

3. *Don't Settle for Safe: Embrace the Uncomfortable to Become Unstoppable* by Sarah Jakes Roberts

4. *How to Sleep Alone in a King-Sized Bed: A Memoir of Starting Over* by Theo Pauline Nester

5. *Dating After Divorce: Getting back into the Game and Starting a New Relationship* by Daytona Watterson

6. *Don't Go in that Room!: A Girlfriend's Guide to Avoiding Dating and Relationship Hell* by Annette Marie Westwood

7. *Mom's House, Dad's House: Making two Homes for Your Child* by Dr. Isolina Ricci

8. *When Mom and Dad Divorce: A Kid's Resource* by R.W. Alley and Emily Menendez-Aponte

9. *My Family is Changing* by Pat Thomas

Knowledge is POWER! You have the POWER to gain as much knowledge as you desire. So, don't stop with the resources provided here; do your own research. Spend time with God, meditate, and listen for His directions for you and your child(ren), so that you are happy and healthy while being single.

## Works Cited

- American Psychological Association, Adapted from Encyclopedia of Psychology. Retrieved from http://www.apa.org/topics/divorce/, May 5, 2018.

- Burke, B.L.J, 7 Stages of Grief During and After Divorce, Divorce Magazine.com, divorcemag.com, updated November 21, 2018

**Where do you find your POWER?**

My POWER is in my Creator. He has given me the all power and authority in every area of my life. I can overcome any obstacle that I face.

# CHAPTER 3

## SAY GOODBYE TO TOXIC RELATIONSHIPS

### By Mia Thomas

---

After 20 years of marriage to the father of my three adult children, I had finally been granted what I had been whining to God about for years... "a divorce." We weren't on the same page in life anymore. I was working long hours to pay the bills and take care of the family, and he was spending his spare time on the couch playing video games. I had fallen out of love with him. I was exhausted, and staying together was no longer an option for me. I had given up; he wanted to keep trying, but I was ready to leave.

My ex and I met when I was in high school, and I was fascinated by having an older military man interested in me. As a rebellious teenager, I was trying to find myself and fighting with the pressure to fit in, while I secretly battled with low self-esteem. I thought he was the answer I needed. Pregnant at 17, he urged me to get my high school diploma, as that was the only way he would marry me. I do credit him in persuading me to get my life back on track -who knows what decisions I would have made if he hadn't given me that ultimatum.

Packing up all my belongings, and never looking back, I was starting my life over. I was finally single and starting a new chapter. A new beginning is what some would call it, a fresh start is what I called it. It was my time to do some things differently in my life. I was now a single mother living on one income with three adult children. I had one child living at home and getting ready to graduate from high school, and two were in college. I will never forget that moment when reality finally hit, and I felt alone. I felt like a failure.

It wasn't long after the divorce I found myself caught up in another relationship. "Mr. Right Now" and I started out working as business partners on a couple of community events with my organization, and I honestly had no intentions of getting involved with anyone. We started building a friendship, and I put my guard down. Before I realized, it we had become caught up and involved in an intimate relationship. Six months had passed, and I thought he was "the one" as he filled that void of loneliness. He was 31, and I was 41, but age didn't mean anything to us. I felt like the new, Stella— *getting my groove back.*

He was everything I wanted in a man. I was a business owner, and so was he. He was funny, charming and a go-getter, just like me. Those were the positives. Now, the not so positive was "Mr. Right Now" had four small children with two baby mama's (full of drama), a needy ex-girlfriend, and a crazy mother living out her real-life Jerry Springer drama moments all the time. Despite all the extra drama we endured, we still pushed forward in our relationship to try and make it work.

46

Every other month there was some type of foolery: baby mama's calling and fussing about child support; the ex-girlfriend sending text messages and constantly calling him to get his attention, while using her son as a token; his mother really not liking me because she preferred his ex-girlfriend to be with him; my children disliking him and blatantly disrespecting him.

There were many red flags I totally ignored in this relationship. I even ignored the people who loved me the most and attempted to warn me. I found myself getting angry and upset with friends and family, and I convinced myself they did not want to see me happy. I also found myself withdrawing from my loved ones; I was in total denial. As time went by, I felt myself slowly deteriorating. I accepted the things I knew were unethical. I even started to devalue myself; I was just existing. But I was his woman, and he was my man. I remember the day he told me, "If we are still together after two years, I will marry you." I was so excited. I trusted and believed in him; I hoped he was going to be my forever. I was in denial that I was an active "willing" participant in a toxic and emotionally abusive relationship. No matter what I did, I could not run from the fact that there were deep seeded issues in my past that were resurfacing. The guilt, shame, and low self-esteem resurfaced, as I emotionally tried to put a Band-Aid on the hurt that I felt. God had sent people in my life to show me that this was not the right man for me; however, just like some of you have done, or may be doing right now, I ignored those signs. I put a Band-Aid on all the lies I was being told and made excuses after excuses to keep him involved in my life. I put a Band-Aid on my pain and covered my scars. My life was hectic, and I felt like I was on an emotional rollercoaster. One minute I was happy, and the next minute I was sad, and then I was angry. I literally started to make myself sick.

## ⏻ From Bad to Worse

As the days went by, I continued to accept however he treated me. There were times when he would leave our home (we had moved in together) for days at a time and would not call. He rarely answered the phone when I called him, and when he did answer he responded with, "I was asleep," "I needed some time to myself," or "I was chilling." I was angry and frustrated… crying myself to sleep at times… and asking myself, "What did I do? Why didn't he come home? Why would he want to do me this way?" I felt like I was the problem.

As time went by, I did my best to make the relationship work. I tried to communicate with him on all levels, only to feel at times like I was walking on eggshells. When I would ask him about his whereabouts, he would become very offensive, saying I was being negative and disrupting the home. Even still, I had his back and helped him keep his life on track overlooking the times he went to jail and would call me in the wee hours to get him out. But, to no avail, nothing satisfied him.

I had lost focus and put aside what God had given me to do with my ministry in order to help him with his business. At the time his business was failing, and I slaved to revive it back to a thriving state. I was the supportive girlfriend and, in the process of helping to keep his business thriving, I stopped focusing on my dreams.

Before "Mr. Right Now" and I had met, I asked God for a financial increase, so I could create jobs for those in my community.

My ministry that was once thriving and bringing in over $20,000 a month was now dying. God was not pleased when I started putting this man before Him, and I did not like the woman I was seeing in the mirror every day. *Who was I?* I was so confused. As things started to rapidly change in our relationship, I noticed the man I thought I was in love with was no longer the same.

## ⏻ My Wake up Call

I had played the fool for too long. I was offering him wifey duties with only girlfriend benefits. I was faithful for three years, even though he promised marriage after two. It was finally time for me to make a choice; either to continue to hold onto something that was an illusion, or accept the fact that God had something greater for me if I would just surrender and be obedient. It wasn't easy, but it happened. There were times when I felt stuck like I could not move on. I found myself rushing to answer his phone calls and returning to that toxic relationship that I knew was not healthy for me. Ladies, have you ever felt like this? I had developed soul ties with him. Soul Ties are emotional and spiritual connections formed as a bond with another person who unites with you. My soul was now intertwined with his soul, and I was a mess. My emotions were all over the place. I became depressed at times and then I would feel happy again. I struggled with being alone and feared the unknown. I had dreaded this moment—the moment we would say goodbye. I sat at home on the end of my bed with no television, no radio, no children around, and no distractions playing in the background. I felt I had no one to talk to. That night as I sat there with tears running down my face, I asked myself the questions: *Why me? What did I do wrong? Was I not pretty enough?*

All of these questions, circulated in my mind over and over again as I became frustrated, sad, and angry. I had started to hate him. I became upset with myself because I had allowed a man to do this again. As I sat there, God spoke with me. I realized He had allowed this break up to happen because it is what I needed to finally begin to live the life I deserved. After going through such terrible relationships, I began to reflect on how I ended up on that path. As with anything in life, we can pay attention to the warning signs, or we can decide to ignore the signs and be forced to deal with the aftermath of the storm.

As I began to go through my healing process, I learned I had been broken for a long time and that I had never really dealt with the root of my issues. I realized I was not ready to be a wife to anyone, more less ready to be in a committed relationship. I wasn't really in love with who I was. I was clueless of who God had created me to be. It was time for me to peel back the layers and find me.

Do you know that in order to move forward in life, we have to peel back those layers that cover us in order to reveal who we really are? Those layers for me consisted of low self-esteem, promiscuity, anger, teen pregnancy, and behavioral issues. Those were the deep dark issues that I had suppressed because I just wanted them to go away and act as if they never happened. So, like many women, I put them in a box and packed them away for a long time. But, we all need to re-open that box and take a look at what's inside at some point. I had to ask myself some hard, self-check questions.

One of the hardest things to do when you feel as if you are in love is to LEAVE someone. We see the signs of being in a toxic relationship, but we are so obsessed with being in love that we ignore all the warning signs. We make excuses for why the other party is doing what they do. We cover up for all their flaws. We start to accept the things we know are not moral and lower our standards to meet theirs. We walk on eggs shells to keep them from being angry.

I am going to list some signs that define if you are in a TOXIC Relationship". If you see yourself in any of these, do yourself a favor and get out of the relationship now:

- Sign 1: You feel drained constantly. It feels as if you are on an emotional rollercoaster. One day you are happy, and the next day you are mad, then the next day you are in tears, and now you are back to happy again. Stop allowing the other person to confuse your emotions.
- Sign 2: There is no trust. For example, he is secretly making or accepting phone calls, text messages, and/or social media messages; he has a social media page and does not accept you as a friend; or, he gets offensive when you ask him about his whereabouts.
- Sign 3: There is a lack of communication. For example, you are always the one who attempts to communicate about a matter-at-hand, or he avoids communication altogether, or has one-sentence conversations.
- Sign 4: There is always drama; it never ends; it's an ongoing story. For example, two or more baby mama's who constantly attempt to call him for no reason regarding issues that do not pertain to his children.
- Sign 5: He always takes and never gives. If you are the one who is always giving in the relationship, and he does nothing but receive all the time, it's TOXIC!

- Sign 6: He is a controlling person. For example, he is dominating and attempts to overpower you. Pay close attention to the warning signs, such as: overreacting, jealousy, and making accusations. Also pay attention if he makes a big fuss about you having time alone. For example, he's constantly calling your phone and questioning your whereabouts. If he isolates you from other people whom you are close to like family, best friends, church or organization members, or he blatantly forbids you to be around the people you love as a requirement for him to stay in the relationship, that's a bad sign. Always remember, real love doesn't have conditions or requirements. You just have to be you.
- Sign 7: He is physically and/or emotionally abusive. If he is putting his hands on you or calling you out of your name, this is totally unacceptable!
- Sign 8: He is continuously being disrespectful. He stays out late at night, not coming home, or calling to let you know his whereabouts.

The list can go on and on. However, when you start to recognize the signs, don't make excuses. It's time to let go. Yes; it will hurt, but only temporarily. You may be asking yourself when do I call it quits? That's a great question! No one can tell you when to QUIT! However, I do believe you have to be so sick and tired that you want to leave. You have to get tired of looking at the broken you in mirror, go to God, and tell him that you are sorry. Ask Him to mend your soul and to help you to break all ties.

There are some things you will have to break in order to move through the healing process. It's time to stop putting a Band-Aid on your wounds and deal with them before they become infected. **You have to get so sick and tired of repeating the cycle that you are willing to fight for yourself.** You have to be in survival mode. What does that look like? Glad you asked.

I remember when I went on a seven-day cruise to Cozumel, Belize, and Honduras. I was so excited that I wanted to try something new, and I mustered up enough courage to go parasailing. I was thousands and thousands of feet in the air. I felt free as a bird—no worries or cares. I felt a peace and calmness. Now, since I cannot swim, I had a life jacket on. As I was in the air, I was very relaxed, until there was a shift in the parachute. A strong wind had caught the parachute and twisted it. Before I knew it, I had fallen so hard that I went underwater. I will never forget that feeling; I thought I was going to lose my life. I was deep underwater, fighting for my life. There were so many things that flashed before me; I didn't know if I would ever get to see my family again. I tried to fight the waves and gasp for air, so that my head would reach above water. I was determined to live because I knew God was not done with me on earth. Thank God, I survived.

When you end a toxic relationship, you have to really be ready to fight for yourself, your sanity, and your right to live. You have to be ready to release yourself from all addictions, all negativity, and all strongholds in order to move forward. You will have to be ready to press through the pain. Yes, it will hurt. Yes, you will cry—over and over again. Yes, you will feel angry, frustrated, irritated, depressed, and very upset with yourself for allowing the other party to hurt you the way that they did. But, you have to realize you will be okay. You have to encourage yourself. You have to forgive yourself and understand that you allowed some things to happen in that toxic relationship because there were no boundaries established in the beginning. Once you get to the stage where you are ready for survival, you will be ready to push forward.

You also must purge from the relationship, and get him out of your system. Webster defines this as: "rid of an unwanted feeling, memory, or condition, typically giving sense of cathartic release". It's time to flush it out your system. Flush out those people, places, environments, and/or circumstances that meant you no good. You also need to break all ties and ALL forms of communication, including deleting all phone numbers, deleting all pictures that lead up to memories, and throwing away all items that will be a reminder of the person. If you are living together pack up all your belongings, and leave as soon as you can. Then, try to find you another place to start over. If you have family and friends available, reach out for their assistance. You never know who is willing to help you. Also, do not answer phone calls or text messages from the person, or lurk on their social media page to see what they're doing, where they're doing it, and who they're doing it with. It is no longer any of your business. Through your detox, be real with yourself. This is not a time to sit in guilt, but to find your freedom. Ask yourself these questions:

1. What is the most challenging thing that is causing me to delay my detox process?

2. Do I choose happiness or leave it to chance?

3. What would happen if I forgave him/her/them?

4. If I stay on the current trajectory, where will I end up? Am I ok

with that?

5. When I look at my life as a whole, what do I think is my main purpose for being in this world? Am I living that out that purpose?

6. What do I most love about myself, and how am I showing that to the world every day?

**You've got to know who you are, know who created you, and know who you belong to.**

It's time to start getting to know you. Start to date yourself. It's time for you to love the woman you see every day in the mirror. Speak positive words of affirmation to yourself. Write the words down on a piece of paper, and post them where you frequent the most. For example, on your night stand, in your favorite book or magazine, on the dashboard in your car, on your refrigerator, in your bathroom by the mirror, etc.

**⏻ What did I learn about myself after my divorce?**

If you were in a situation like I was, I want you to take some time to reflect, and answer these questions as well:

- What does the root of my problem stem from?

- This is the time when you stop and truly look in the mirror. Do a self-evaluation, and see who you really are. Take inventory. Make changes to what you do not like.

- When someone sees your name on Caller ID, what thoughts

and feelings do you want them to have? What are you doing to create those?

Lastly, now that you have gone through your healing process, it time for your final goodbyes. Let go, accept, and understand that he was not the man for you. Next, accept that your season with him is over. You had some good and some bad memories, but it's time to move forward. Then, set a timeframe and give yourself a time limit when you will no longer keep talking about him. Stop reliving what used to be. Lastly, write a goodbye letter expressing how you feel and how he hurt you. It is time to say goodbye. When you complete it, put the letter in an envelope and do not mail it. This letter will be addressed to who you are walking away from and what you are walking away from. Seal this letter in an envelope, address it, then rip it up and throw it way. Let's give it a try.

Dear _____,

Describe how you felt about them.

_____

_____

_____

_____

Describe how you were hurt by them.

_____

_____

_____

_____

Describe how they made you feel by hurting you.

_____

_____

_____

_____

As of this day, I have prayed and asked God to forgive me for anything I may have done wrong as well. But most of all, I asked Him to heal my mind and my soul, and to totally release me from this toxic relationship. I wish you well in whatever you do. As of this day forward, I AM FREE!

GOODBYE TO TOXIC RELATIONSHIP(S),

Your Name,

_____

**Where do you find your POWER?**

When I see the smiles on my children's faces, while simply sitting around the house; I'm reminded that what I'm doing is working. It gives me strength.

# CHAPTER 4

## GUILT-FREE MOTHERHOOD

### By Brittany R. Hatcher

———————◈———————

You couldn't have paid me to believe I'd be a single mother… twice. I thought I'd learned my lesson the first go around. *How could someone who had so much going for herself fall twice for men who weren't ready for a future with her?* I thought to myself. Well, really neither of us was ready and to their credit, I never asked the right questions. I was a young mother; my journey started at 17. From the day my belly bulged, folks would stare and chatter. I always looked younger than I actually was with my petite frame and my baby face. The only weight I really had was baby weight. So, maybe strangers were staring because I looked like a pregnant 12-year-old, while the people who knew me… well, they were staring so they could "run and tell that." Eventually came the warnings (some spoken and some suggested) of just how hard single "mommy hood" would be, how fast I'd have to mature, and most importantly how the world was no longer my oyster. I started to believe the negativity. For some crazy reason, I actually believed everyone who diminished single parenthood to a life of poverty, neglect, and depression.

The thing is, for 17 years I'd believed the total opposite about myself. For 17 years, I'd believed that skin color, location, and lack of money couldn't stop me from being great. So, how could nine months change my whole existence? The day I stopped believing statistics determined my path is the day success started creeping in on me. Slowly, but surely, I'm rocking this thing labelled as "single motherhood," even if it started off rocky.

## ⏻ I wasn't ready to be a mother

Coming home with a child strapped to a heart monitor wasn't an easy transition. Going from pregnant teen to nursing a sick born baby wasn't the least bit glamorous. Every cable show that "taught" me what to expect [during birth and delivery] was the total opposite of my pre and postpartum life. I wasn't prepared to birth my son two months early, see him strapped to machines, nor leave him behind at the hospital. Leaving him at the hospital was probably the second most frustrating and frightening feeling I'd had to date. Realizing that I was actually in labor was the first. But you have to understand, I was living in my mom's house, and my pregnancy already had us in a weird space. Expressing my needs and emotions wasn't an option. I would have been met with "*I told you so's,*" when what I needed most was a hug.

I also wasn't ready for recurring medical treatments, prescriptions, nor running back and forth to the emergency room. I legit didn't know what to do with a baby who wasn't supposed to be born yet. The machine... and the medicine... and the crying for no reason... and the nursing combined with the time limit I gave myself to figure it all out, had me on eggshells. I think I ran out of tears.

Hopeful parents and newlyweds often try to "ready themselves" for parenthood. Couples tend to babysit nieces and nephews and such to get a "feel" for parenting. It's different when the buck stops at you, though; it brings a different type of pressure. That's what it felt like— unbridled pressure. The pressure of ME thinking I was the reason he was a sick baby, I was the reason he was born early, I was the reason we didn't have any money- as I tried to make my Taco Bell check stretch, and I was the reason he didn't have a daddy around. How was I supposed to to raise him to be a whole man? It was all too much pressure! I started doubting myself on day one by worrying about 18 years of life rather than parenting one day at a time. And to be honest, that same damaging thought process held me captive up until a few years ago.

Years leading up to my pregnancy weren't really baby-filled. My brother was 10 years my junior; waking up some nights to feed and play with him was voluntary. Although I enjoyed those impromptu moments, parenthood was now mandatory. Well, it was for me anyway. I quickly learned why God designed children to be born to a married couple instead of a fornicating teenager. Amidst the ongoing transition I had to own my reality, and although additional family members would help when asked, the bulk of parenting responsibility fell on me. It was my responsibility to own or to whine about. Honestly, I did both.

Owning responsibility can be scary, frustrating, and tiring in itself. Bottled emotions and unsolved frustrations will always affect a person's daily life. Needless to say, I wasn't always the nicest "baby mama." And by the time I got into the rhythm of apparent sole responsibility, I wasn't too keen on impromptu fathering either.

Sometimes, parents don't take time to put themselves in the others' shoes. I wish we did; I wish they could have seen the worn-out person behind the scowl. The scowl that came from jealousy; jealousy of the carefree dad life—or so it seemed. Dads could pop up, have a fun weekend/summer (if they opted to), then drop the unevenly-shared responsibility (child) back off for me to be Dr. Jekyll and Mrs. Hyde with. I had to be the disciplinarian when needed and smiling cover-tucker at night whether the boys had a good or bad day—all in the same day. Keeping my game face on while figuring out if I was being too harsh or too lenient was a constant struggle among other things. I honestly hate thinking back to some of the years of their childhood. I simply didn't understand how both impromptu parents made the same physical decision, got the same result, yet the buck ultimately stopped at me. Couple this unsolved mystery with the reality that I still [to this day] hadn't met my biological dad, and you'll get my want, well sometimes overzealous need, to create more shared responsibility with their dads. I know; I know. They had a village. I should have reached out to the village. The early years were iffy, though. Things went on that only us parents know; yet, everyone had an opinion. When you have children young eeeeeevvveeerryone has an opinion.

There were times I was emotionally drowning and just didn't speak up. I mean, saying something would have been either perceived as a pity party, or demonizing their dad(s). An emotional support system was definitely lacking in my life, and unfortunately not something discussed in my family or culture most of the time. "Pray about it, or you need Jesus," summed up that area of support. So, why didn't I ask around for more help? It's a nice thought, but people don't always hear the comments being made when help is rendered, nor the guilt behind having to ask and/or knowing you had to. I'd much rather

62

work myself into the ground than have someone throw support in my face, or talk behind my back, about something they did for me and/or for the boys. This reality quickly morphed me into the person who felt like she had to do most things alone.

As you can probably tell, parent life was a bit rocky in the earlier years. I don't know when my anger started subsiding, or when I became more sensible about it all. I don't know when I finally realized that fussing, yapping, and arguing wasn't changing a thing. However, I do know our children hold a special place in our hearts. It's inexplicable how life can go from being "all about you" to being "all about them." I remember being shocked at the reality that I was going to have a real live baby. All moms have their own take on motherhood, but most can agree that babies are pure miracles. At some point during both pregnancies, I shut out the "but you're not married comments," and focused on the joy that was coming. I didn't know about baby expenses, if my relationships with their fathers would be rekindled, or if I was mentally ready for motherhood or much anything else. But, somehow, I knew things would work for our good.

Years down the line, I can look back and realize their dads were the same "not ready for this" that I was. I just happened to be the parent with the physical reminder that our baby was on the way. I had to answer the hard questions, sign up for this program, go to all the doctors' appointments, etc. I didn't have a pause button. If only I knew then what I know now.

I used to get so antsy when I had to make fast decisions for my mini family. I remember getting to the second week of college midterms… or maybe they were finals. My oldest wasn't walking yet, and I was having trouble with daycare almost weekly. I'd filed for daycare assistance through the government, but also worked part-time when not in class. Somehow, someway, my $8 an hour for a few hours a week was too much money to receive daycare benefits *some* weeks. Luckily, my son has some amazing family members who soon started babysitting him at the drop-of-a-hat when I needed it. Soon the two jobs, college class life, and my new thirst for going out to finally have fun (I was a pretty sheltered kid), caught up to me when I needed to cram for finals. Somehow, I digested most of the info. My son was being watched by family, and I was ready for the next day of tests. Then, my car stopped. I freaked out. I had to get another one. I didn't think about carpooling, or borrowing money, or figuring out the bus system, or anything like that. I was a quick, irrational decision maker. I was already receiving help in the form of daycare; I didn't want to ask for anything else. I surely wasn't going to miss, or potentially be late for, my finals. So there I was at the costly, overpriced, high mileage, car lot signing my finances away for an old vehicle that solved my problems for a few months. All I knew was that I had to keep the momentum of college "working for me" because from the time I knew I was pregnant, chaos ensued.

Attending college was a huge game-changer for me. The fact that my son could go to school with me, have child care (most of the time), and we could live off $180 in food stamps for four years was a step in the right direction. It gave me time to think and process what in the world had really happened. I could be a "big kid" for a little while and hopefully map out a future without the world breathing down my neck. Leaving my comfort zone of a neighborhood, although only two hours away, was good for my assumed freedom. I can't think straight when I don't see an "out." Staying at home, I didn't see a way out. I just saw this pregnant girl making minimum wage arguing with her mom. College was the light at the end of the tunnel for me. I had to make it work.

College/mama/employee life became easier over time but was still overwhelming. Forced repetition can be overwhelming. I wanted to be young and carefree so badly. And when I made non-mom/non-student decisions, I definitely paid for them. My emotions still weren't balanced in several areas, and I continued to wonder about next week, next month, and next year while totally missing the beauty of the current day.

I had led myself to believe I was "on my own" in so many ways—from the animosity between me and my mom that seemed to get worse when I got pregnant, to the reality of being a single mom, to coming to grips with my dad not wanting to be in my life, to putting my son in a situation where he wouldn't have both of his parents in the same household. I felt like I had to fix everything and iron it all out myself. This mentality became my lifestyle. Don't get me wrong; there's a positive side to this "all of nothing" mindset. I definitely set and reached goals, made sure my boys were okay, and was able to prepare for some of the pitfalls that came my way. Anxiety that I may not be able to handle a surprise hurdle was also part of this mindset.

My do-it-by-myself, short-end-of-the-stick attitude turned mantra was no good at team projects in school or work, for that matter. Needless to say, I have a very dominant disposition that didn't fare well in my dating life. This mindset took me down long paths for no reason. Although I had the benefit of knowing things would get done when I needed them to, I also perfected the danger of isolation. I totally overlooked the possibility of carpooling, sisterhood, rekindling relationships, etc. over time. I was the epitome of "if you want something done you have to do it yourself."

I'm sure you agree that life, to this point, was somewhat chaotic. Progress was being made in some areas, but issues were being born in others. There was always something to fix, to figure out, or to pay for. There was never enough time in the day. And when I took a break from trying to stay above water, I felt bad for leaving all the unsolved issues behind. That's how I felt most of the time. I soon became unable to focus on goals because I was always fixing something the fast and wrong way. I can't tell you how many smiles and "you're doing so good's" I heard while making the worst decisions of my life and getting involved with people I had no business saying a word to. People never see the whole picture, but will make a determination based on what they want it to be—good or bad.

It took years to realize I can only control one variable in most situations—me. It took years to change my approach to people, issues, and figuring out what was next. I learned to give my brain rest in the midst of everything going on. (My close friends laugh at me because they know I'll grab my blanket and take a nap in the middle of a tsunami.) Naturally, my woman genes made me replay scenarios through my mind and come up with a quick solution. But I'd done that before, and I'd failed at it. I didn't pray about it. I didn't give myself time to meditate on it. I didn't look around and see what my options were. Giving myself a minimum of 24 hours "chill time" before making decisions has now made a huge difference. Problems just seem so much easier to conquer after a bubble bath and a little

Moscato in my system. You live and learn.

I've heard myself say over and over how I wasn't ready to have my now 15-year-old son. However, seeing the words "fifteen-year-old son" written out makes me better accept why I was always in a rush to build a good life, even at the expense of my peace and enjoyment. Besides, we are never 100% ready for anything. There's always a learning curve and a lesson to digest. So, at some point, I stopped beating myself up for all the mistakes I made in their younger years and hope to grow in all areas as I mature.

The demands of life don't let up because you're a mom, employee, student, business owner or whatever. Bills are still due, and hurdles stay sneaking up on a sister… but my attitude towards these things has changed. Every issue doesn't have to be a disaster—even if it's a surprise. There are lots of things my still "green-to-life" self can be prepared for. I can be ready for impromptu expenses that come with home ownership. I can keep up my car's maintenance (oil changes at a minimum). I can even schedule regular mini-pampering sessions to ensure I get necessary "me time" regardless of how life's treating me at the moment. I'm one of those people who talks to themselves, strategizes out loud, and writes everything down. When I'm hit with challenges, I easily escalate a mole hill into a mountain if I don't stay centered, calm, and enter a quiet place to rest and think. It's amazing the positivity that comes when you're alone and giving yourself the ability to problem solve. During these quiet sessions, I'm reminded of all the things I've conquered before. If I did it once, I can definitely do it again. And no matter how frustrated or end-of-the-worldish I felt before, I wasn't broken. So whatever I could be currently facing, or will face, simply doesn't have the fortitude to break me. Once I incredible hulk up my thoughts, I can easily plan a rise from any downfall. Perspective changes everything; improved perspective mandates a better outcome.

### ⏻ It's one of me

The first few years of single mommy-hood were spent re-explaining myself over and over again. I was constantly trying to change the look of pity that came over the face of strangers when they learned it was "just me" and my sons. "You're doing well... for a single mother," or "he speaks really well," or "he has such great manners." I won't lie; I take offense when people sound surprised and give sideways compliments that my children can speak well, hold the door open for ladies, use proper manners, etc. The compliments are most likely 100% genuine, but my struggle to be "enough" of everything haunts me daily. *Did I teach them correctly? There's a lady standing up, and there are no seats; hopefully, one of the boys offers theirs. Did he say thank you? Did he say please?* Eventually I laid down the offense and anxiety of hoping my children would regurgitate my expectations. And when I did, I started to notice something amazing—that my *best* was enough.

As the years progressed, I wore the single parent label like an ill-gotten badge of honor. It's easy to get slightly big-headed when you finally start progressing in an area you struggled with for years. This self-proclaimed badge didn't help much of anything. It sure didn't help my strained dating life. Yes; you read right. I had the nerve to try to add dating to an already chaotic equation. If raising two boys in a single-parent household wasn't intimidating enough on its own, I felt like I needed to hurry up and be someone's wife.

Oh, the pressure of love and marriage! If I had a boyfriend for longer than a millisecond folks would frequently ask if we were getting married. And if the answer was no, or probably not, then came the time frame question. "Well, when are you going to get married?" Subtle or bold family and friends would remind me of the "need" to have a man in my son's lives, the blessing of having a two-parent household, and more but didn't think about three main facts:

1. Maybe I wasn't ready.
2. Maybe the men I'd come across weren't husband—or better yet—MY husband material.
3. And just perhaps, maybe, I was supposed to focus on me and my family for the time being.

It took me almost 30 years of living, and 13 years of parenthood, to realize it's okay to chart my own path. I'm not married, and I don't' know when I will be. I don't want to share my closet, or a bank account, or much else on most days. Some nights, I want to sleep on the couch just so I don't have the fold the clothes on my bed. And if I drink too much wine while binging a show in the bathtub all night, I just may not Ajax the tub's dirt ring til morning… or afternoon. And, I'm fine with that.

My not-right-now attitude towards marriage means there is just one of me. Singular. Uno. THERE IS JUST ONE OF ME, AND THAT'S OKAY! Society is not going to force me into marriage just because it's the thing to do. I've accepted that I'm not ready to merge my boys into the responsibility that marriage brings. Early isn't always good. We don't want people to die early, eat half-cooked food, or have children early. And, I'm not getting married early. Nope! Not jumping into something I'm not ready for. I'm enough by myself. The last time I entered a relationship prematurely, I ended up being a single mom. There's one of me; one mom. And although there's nothing wrong with my reality, there's sacrifice involved.

Since my boys live with me, I do and will always bear more responsibilities than their dads do. It's just reality. When something happens at school, I get the call. If a program is cancelled, and my son needs a ride home, I have to leave my pre-planned engagement to pick him up. If they wake up sick in the middle of the night, I have to take his temperature, lay him in the bed next to me, and clean up the vomit that's sure to come. I'm going to continue to be the human taxi traveling from all sides of town to deliver one to practice and the other to a game only to repeat the trips at pick up. It's a hard knock life, but one of us have to do it. The reality is the dad and I parted ways, and since my sons stayed with me, the buck stops at me. Years later I stopped complaining about the responsibility that comes with being the custodial parent. I could have saved all the yapping.

One day when I was playing taxi cab, I had a long overdue epiphany. My oldest was late to something, and I'd missed a school event for the youngest and felt very bad about it. I'd been at work all day helping and counseling other children and forgot to support my own. But truth is, I couldn't do it all.

I finally accepted there was just one of me, and all I could do was my best. And my best just had to be good enough. Years later I stopped trying to compensate for a two-parent household and started giving my son everything I could possibly give: one singular capable and loving mom.

This long overdue revelation led me to also accept that my family of three was just fine. I didn't need to explain to folks why their dads weren't in the household, nor did I need to compete with other families. Here I was in tears every time a "Donuts for Dads" event flier came home, meanwhile my kids were just fine with me showing up looking mom-ly.

I distinctly remember standing in my kitchen doing one of the zillions of chores that never seemed to stay done. I was bantering to myself about the frustrations of having to figure out my schedule for the next day and basically frustrated with having to be two places at one time. I didn't want the youngest to miss his program 'cause the oldest had somewhere to be. I was visibly frustrated when my son walked in and asked what was wrong. I ranted my adult vent list that I'm sure went over his head. I ended with, "I just can't do it all." He responded, "Well, just do what you can, Mom. Want to watch a show?" My whole face dropped. That was the day my outlook changed... the day I became a better mom... a better me... and the day I became enough.

He was right. There was no sense muttering about what I couldn't do; I needed to shift focus to what I was able to accomplish. Granted, watching a TV show with him didn't solve my next day scheduling problems, but it did give my running mind a break. He said so much in those few words; his simple statement reminded me that things were okay—my boys were okay. They were happy, and they were loved. They wanted and needed a human mom—not an octopus unsuccessfully doing a lot and making no progress. In so many words, he reminded me that my family of three was fine as is. He reminded me that I didn't need to beat myself up over being unable to do everything. I don't know where I picked up the Super Mom cape, or why I felt the need to own one, but my boys weren't concerned with it. They wanted what I wanted in reverse. Just like I wanted—needed—them to be happy, they wanted the same for me.

This new realization meant I couldn't be everywhere, and they couldn't do everything. Sometimes our schedules clashed and still do. I drag my youngest to a lot of things he doesn't want to go to; my oldest is used to napping in the car when I have evening meetings and such. And yep, those are my kids you'll probably have to step over because I'm working an event and don't have time to go home before their seasonal sports games. And nope, there isn't anyone else who can remotely keep up with our schedule of drop offs and pick-ups… because some days I'm figuring out the plan of attack while driving to Point A. So to the coaches, that means my kids won't be at every practice, rehearsal, event, etc. We're going to miss out on some things and choose what's most important. But, you know what? That's just fine. I had to make it fine. I had to make everyone else be okay with how WE needed to function to maintain our own happiness and peace. To sum all of this up, we are a functional family of three, and we do what works for us. Function isn't about everyone else; it's about what works for you and yours.

The day I stopped measuring our effectiveness based on the cookie-cutter family we aren't was the day life got 10 times easier.

⏻ **I'm the boss**

It's the age of social media and, nine times out of 10, a tech savvy millennial's Facebook or Instagram feed will feature what's important to them. You'll find my boys smiling faces up and down my feed every time they do something regular that moms tend to label extraordinary. And somewhere under the pictures, or in my phone's text box, you'll find a family member asking why I didn't tell them about an event. This short letter is for you.

*Dear Everybody,*

*I'm a single mama of two boys who's also running a business, trying to have some sort of a dating life and, up until writing this, has worked full-time (and sometimes two and three jobs) to keep life decent. This also means I can't keep up with everything. I mean, I can… but not necessarily by everyone else's time constraints.*

*Understand that at the time I "check in" to one of the kid's events on social media that most, if not all, of the following things are evident:*

- *I've left one of the lights on in my house; yet, I complain about the bill daily.*

- *The dog either has food OR water, rarely both at the same time.*

- *Either both my legs are shaved, or my woman-stache is (one or the other, not both).*

- *I don't know what we're eating for dinner.*

- *I haven't checked the mail in days.*

- *There's expired food in my fridge.*

- *I missed an appointment, or an event, or something… had to.*

- *I'm mad at myself because I ate something that I said I wasn't going to eat.*

- *I'm just trying to keep up.*

It seems, at times, I don't have my life together. I always say there's not enough time in the day; yet, I don't want more of it because I'd still have to balance life accordingly. My mind literally stays running all day long from business thoughts to family vacays, and other things I don't have time to conquer. I'm sure I'm not the only one but, hey, I'm effective when it matters most.

It's amazing how much power the mind has over what's perceived to be situations beyond our control. All the time I spent feeling like I couldn't be an effective single mom to two will-be-black men was also the time my household was a wreck in every way. There I was focusing on what I *couldn't* change while believing every negative stereotype ever said or written. There I was with the roadmap that women before me had paved, yet I wasn't being positive. Soon enough, I became the boss of my happiness.

You know what? That felt good. Somehow throughout my little roller coaster life of changes, I forgot I'm the boss; I'm the leader. I had to own the need to take care of myself, speak life to myself, and allow myself to do what works for us. I can even hear myself saying, "Well, you know how it is when you have kids; they come first." And yeah that sounds good, y'all. It has a nice little cliché ring to it but if they're always first, and I'm always last, who's leading? Who's in control? Who's setting an example for those to follow behind? Slowly, but surely, I'm rearranging my spot within my own existence and doing whatever works for us unapologetically.

I'm an observant person. I make mental notes when I'm out people-watching. I'll run into high school classmates, and we all have had our share of "life"—some married, some single, some divorced, etc. But for the most part, many are raising children. When I see moms who look worn, torn, and beat down, I get it. I understand it. I look at some of my own pictures from time to time and wonder what in the world was attacking me at that moment. Or, better yet, *What did I choose to let conquer me?"*

I lived like other people felt I should for so long and still failed at that. I gained so much weight, my skin suffered, my attitude suffered, and many times couldn't think straight. I set ridiculous goals for myself while telling other people they need to slow down. I put so much unrealistic pressure on my life, my looks, my relationships, and my progress.

Funny how perspective changes everything. Now that I actually believe I'm good enough as is, I still have areas that need improvement. I'm just okay with improving them at my own pace. I'm the chunkiest, puffiest person typing this right now because I'm behind on the deadline. And either I can save the last few hours of daytime power-walking the neighborhood trying to earn a cookie, or I can put pen to paper. I've learned to choose what's most important to me. The therapeutic release I get when writing allows me to be free-minded when I do other things. Perhaps, I'll enjoy my jog a bit more once I'm done with this chapter.

I finally learned to take charge and only do what's important to me at this point in my life. We all have life organized based on what's important whether we acknowledge it or not. Even our simplest traditions can be self-inflicted or based on someone else's ideologies. I'm all about breaking down my thoughts and doing what I want to do from now on. Either I can stop for gas or be home to see my favorite show begin. I can save money by cooking what's in the deep freezer, or I can grab some fast food and be a couch potato a little earlier than expected. The same can be said for the more difficult/important decisions I've had to make over the last year. It's okay to give yourself wiggle room every now and then.

My new attitude soon affected my work life. My goal had always been to climb the education ladder and retire from the school District as the head of some department. I mean everyone wants to "make it to the top" of their profession, career, ministry, etc. People may not want the responsibility that comes with progression, but we all have a hint of competition in our being. My professional path took a detour, and it was the best thing that could have happened to/for me. I still want to climb the ladder, but I want it to be my own ladder. I'm all about making it to the next level, as long as I don't have to compromise my time and freedom.

If you were to meet me right now, you might be a little put off by my "only doing what I want to do" attitude. This month marks so much transition for me—quitting a career in education, going full-time with my business, seeing real growth and contentment in my long-distance relationship, and ultimately... finally realizing there's truth to the cliché phrase that I can be whatever I want to be when I grow up.

I graduated high school when there was a huge national urgency for minorities and women to enter the science realm. Following this trend and unfounded promise, I studied chemistry. College-level chemistry was much different than the internships I breezed through in high school, and I quickly learned being a closed door buttoned up in a lab coat just wasn't for me. But then came the "realism" and doubting voice I'd heard so many times before reminding me that dreams don't always equal a paycheck, and a degree meant I could at least make rent. What a minimalist I used to be! There I was working towards a degree in something I was "good at" but never really wanted to do.

My biology degree led me to a couple of positions that allowed me to showcase my fun side and pretty much talk to people all day. Yeah, I know, being a receptionist couldn't take care of my family, but it reminded me that a job didn't have to be boring and consuming. Over the last 10 years my positions in education ranged from supporting one campus to nine, and from a list of students to targeted families. I found myself in an overwhelming position of frustration. Here I was trying my best to help students struggling to meet pre-set education standards; yet, they all had different foundations. I grew an attachment to families and their struggles. I took their struggles home with me. There I was trying to attack non-education problems while working inside an educational entity, all the while, being rated based on whether or not a student could pass the next standardized test coming their way.

I don't know when I had enough of it. I've always cared about other people and found myself playing devil's advocate when needed: "But have you tried this or that," or "You have to stay positive," or a host of other slogans I've adopted. "Write your goals down," or a famous one I don't use anymore, "Don't worry about it; I'll take care of it."

I allowed support roles to overextend my emotions, my own family's time, and my happiness. "People work" is so draining. Don't get me wrong; it's rewarding and necessary, but it's so easy to get your heartstrings tangled up into someone else's needs. I looked up one day and realized I'd been putting more effort into other folks' families causing mine to suffer. I'd had enough.

I was always exhausted. After a few months of being reassigned to work for a terribly unhappy supervisor, I knew I was at the end of my rope. I had a family to support and although my business was doing well, I wasn't confident enough to choose me/us. I say that because we are all capable of amazing things with the right motivation. Working in a toxic environment was the push I needed to become my own boss.

I'd always been a serial shopper and a serial eater when it came to handling problems. There was no issue a double serving of peach cobbler and a new purse couldn't fix. Neither of those options were smart, and pretty soon I had more clothes than I could fit in my closet. Working for the local school district meant the workforce was predominantly female; most women love to shop. I remember wearing a dress to work one day that someone fell in love with. In a joking manner I replied that everything I owned was for sale, and I'd wash and deliver it the next day. The next day she asked for the dress, but I didn't have it. I was joking. I turned that joke into a business.

It took a few years of delivering "cute cases" of clothing to people and customers making late payments for me to realize I needed an actual clothing store to sustain my idea. It took renting a few spaces for me to figure out I didn't want to "have to be present" at any certain time to sell any certain thing. Enough weekends away from the boys and begging people to work my rental space opened up the world of e-Commerce for me. Thrifting had always been a hobby, and eyeing quality items came easy for me. Fast forward to a grant ending position and the need to focus on own family—it's now my primary source of income. Although I grew comfortable with my monthly salary, I wanted my freedom. I needed to be my own boss for a while—in every way possible. I needed to make drastic changes that would reset my life and my mind. Leaving behind a career in education and focusing on a business that made me happy changed my perspective on life.

These last few months of very loose preparation for running a resale business havegiven me so much hope for the future. I've been a better mom, and I've ultimately decided to pay more attention to myself. My aches that cause me to "need" a massage, my headaches that mean I need to take a vacation to relax, the scars on my face that mean I need to pay more attention to my food intake are high priorities now. I'm a priority now.

Being the boss is often referred to when discussing a job's role; but I'm finally accepting that I can be the mom boss of myself, my kids, and our lives… and I don't have to sacrifice success to do it. Some women can do it all—have the career, manage the house, and flourish! I'm not her—at least not right now—and I'm okay with that. And being okay with my decisions have become one of the most peaceful ways to live life for me.

## ⏻ I don't know everything

"I accept my situation for what it is," is an easy statement to voice, but is not always easy to digest. Accepting my role as a single mom and head of household meant I was accepting a host of other realities like:

- *Primary financial responsibility;*

- *Primary emotional stability responsibility;*

- *Primary decision-making responsibility; and,*

- Basically *the Wizard of Oz, as far as my kids were concerned.*

Kids are emerging from the womb ready to jump into technology; I wouldn't be surprised if their first word was "Why?" In the year 2019, at least this seemed to be the case for my boys. They wanted to know why things are the way they are; an answer wasn't good enough if proof wasn't attached to it. Access to fast-paced technology is a plus and minus when raising children. The internet makes research easy and can teach the most rudimentary person the hardest tasks if given time. This fast-paced access to answers doesn't yield much practice for situations in life that require patience, emotional leverage, and room for human error. We're trying to physically hug kids that would rather send a kiss via Instagram.

It's safe to say my boys have learned that Siri is much smarter than I am. I don't have the answer to everything. Having my sons young meant they have watched me grow alongside them. I've fussed when I should have listened and punished them out of sheer frustration when a simple conversation would have probably fixed the moment. There have been mornings I woke up and apologized to the big brown-eyed boys who were simply being kids in a moment when their mama needed a break and couldn't have one. That's when I realized yet another mistake I was consistently making. When I was clocking waaaaayy too many hours in my never-ending single mother work week, I would turn into this harping Tasmanian devil who would spew for at least five minutes about what wasn't clean, how there weren't enough hours in the day, and so on. When I think about my actions and words now, it's clear as day; I was having adult tantrums. When I think about the many times I raged and ranted—I didn't have to. It wasn't that serious, and I created an atmosphere of uneasiness throughout our home. Fast forward to current day, and the reality is my boys understand my need for alone time. They understand that their completed chores mean mama can focus on the family's life obstacles that surface each month. All I had to do was tell them. My boys became better children the second I became a better mom. Changing the way I communicated with them made my house a home.

I spent so much time thinking I had to be perfect, look perfect, and be the constant example parent for my boys 100% of the time. I felt like I had to hide all my mistakes and tears from them for some strange reason. Revealing my scars and explaining their role in making our family successful is the epitome of parenting done right in my opinion.

I'm doing things right this time. I'm thinking things through this go around at life. I can be as dynamite as I want to be, and multi-task like the dickens, but there's still just one of me. The one me has always been enough for them. They knew it all along, but I was so busy beating myself up that I didn't realize how comfortable, grateful, and insanely loved they felt.

Even with all of this discovery, self-awareness, and growth I still have times when I literally have to recite positive phrases and write reminder notes to myself. I still close my bedroom door, shut my eyes, and say out loud, "You've got this; they're okay with this arrangement, and you'll figure it out." I constantly remind myself that the little humans I'm working so hard for are more than pleased with what little ol' me has been able to maintain for them even in the times where it's evident I'm still trying to figure out the formula that is effective parenting.

## ⏻ The Mama Defense

One of the biggest keys to figuring out the effective parenting formula was figuring out my place among other moms. I'm human. We have a natural need to be amongst people like us at times—people who understand us and that we have commonalities with. You'd think I'd hit it off with another African-American mom of two boys around about the same age as my boys, right? Perhaps... if she was as single mother.

There was a time in my life when I wouldn't open my mind to even discuss the simplest parenting hacks, funny stories, or worries amongst someone who wasn't in "the single parent club." I'll be honest. I got tired of hearing wives whine about there not being enough time in the day, how expensive daycare was, and how much they wished their money-earning, in-home living, emotionally supportive husbands would help with the kids more often. My eyes are rolling into the back of my head while I type this. I figured there was no way someone who had an in-home support system (whether physical, financial, emotional, or a combination of any) could remotely understand my daily struggle to feel effective. When I wasn't mentally fighting myself, I was creating another divide.

I'd cringe when a military wife would say, "I'm like a single mom when Bill's away with the military." I'd literally leave the area when a wife complained about her husband's excessive business travel during the first few weeks after their child was born. I remember laying on the couch so sore from my c-section that I couldn't move fast enough to catch my, then one-week-old, son from rolling onto the floor. But somehow, I picked him up and rested enough to drive my oldest son to school the next morning. I didn't have the luxury of heeding the doctor's orders or crying on a supportive shoulder. Somewhere between bitterness, regret, self-pity, and my "the world is not fair" attitude derived my angers towards the "supported mom." Since I didn't have those luxuries, I didn't want to be around someone who did. I'm sure I missed out on good girl talk and possibly friendship due to what I realize was pure jealousy. My younger years were filled with so much confusion of how I ended up being a double single mother to begin with. I'd always seen myself as wife—not someone who had to attend child support court to figure out who would cover my sons' health insurance.

To this day my insides turn a bit when I hear moms play like they remotely know what single mom life is—and they've not lived it. But why? Why was I so defensive? Why did I feel the need to debate the topic so much? To air my experience to those I knew hadn't lived the life I had? The reason is because I was jealous and unhappy with what I'd accepted single parenthood to be. Something as small as an application form reminding me that my prefix is "Ms." could trigger a moment of "how did I get here?"

Sure the situation wasn't ideal, and any mom would want a loving, functioning household with Mom and Dad to be part of the equation if possible. My reality was different. The longer it took me to accept my reality, the more I could blame my frustration on others and justify the adult tantrums. None of that was progressive. I finally had to address why someone else's view on their brief stint as a single mom bothered me. Why hearing "Ms." Hatcher instead of "Mrs." made me angry. I finally know the answer. It's because I hadn't accepted my reality for what it was.

Fifteen years ago I was a new mother trying to prove to others I could do this right. My energy was spent on correcting folk's notions that I'd ruined my life, and that all my dreams were now deferred. Not one ounce of me was dedicated to what my current reality proved had always been possible—God-driven success. I've finally accepted my reality and all that comes with it:

- I'm the doctor for them.

- I'm the way they get around.

- I'm going to make errors disciplining them.

- I'm going to have to apologize to them.

- I'm going to cry.

- It may take me a bit longer to single-mindedly figure out issues that come our way, but it will get done.

Most importantly, our family of three is going to continue to be progressive. Identifying personal areas that needed improvement closed the lens I pointed at other people. After doing the grueling much-needed work on myself, I no longer focused on what anyone else thought. I've accepted that I am capable of success, power, and prosperity as long as I stay on my own path. Comparing myself to anyone else—married or single—isn't smart or fair. My reality is that I'm single-handedly the best thing that ever happened to my boys, and they were the reasons for finding my truth:

- I'm going to excel.

- I'm going to stay encouraged.

- I'm going to dominate my reality

## Meet Janet Yarbrough

**Where do you find your POWER?**

Only through the grace of God.

# CHAPTER 5

## FROM ONE SINGLE MOTHER TO ANOTHER

### By Janet Yarbrough

---

I think my background was that of a normal middle-class child. I am the eldest of two children who are more than five years apart; my parents, both recent transplants to Southern California, met in California. They were later married in their early twenties in Washington, DC where I was born while my father was stationed there as an army soldier. Shortly after I was born, they returned to California. My mother stayed home until my brother went to school; even then, she didn't work full-time. My parents bought a new house in an up and coming neighborhood while they were still in their late twenties. They were married for 51 one years before my mother passed; neither of them took the traditional college route, but finished at different levels and were successful in their careers. My brother and I started off at a private school and later evolved to more well-rounded public neighborhood schools.

As a child, I can't remember being taught any special life lessons. I was taught that you can tell a person to go to hell in such a way it might be the next day before they realized what you told them. I remember being taught to go after what I wanted and not to let "them" (whoever them was) tell you no. This served me well during college application time and when moving from my parent's house to buy my first home.

I remember, more often than not, relatives living with us during a transition or difficult periods and holidays where my parents included elderly relatives and neighbors, so they wouldn't be alone. Part of the day was spent with my mother driving around to get them. Likewise, I remember them caring for elderly relatives and taking us after school, with books in hand, because they wouldn't leave us at home alone.

I recall parties for most every occasion, but not necessarily for birthdays. And as we got older, we were taught by my father why understanding and managing finances was important and taught by my mother that everyone deserves a second chance. And, even when I left home, my parents were proudly present at my most important work and community accomplishments.

My late husband, though from a slightly different family life, still came with many similarities. He was the second of six children, all stair-stepped. He was raised in the Midwest, but both of his parents were from Georgia. His parents owned their home, and both worked full-time. His father, the entrepreneur, worked during the day; his mother, the Registered Nurse, worked at night. Though for reasons of their own I'm told, his parents weren't as involved in their kids' activities but their house, like mine, was often open for relatives to stay a while or to move in. During college, he relocated to California and lived with his uncle and aunt for a short time while his parents and the rest of the family remained in Ohio.

And so it was, we met while each of us was attending separate birthday celebrations of our friends. After dating we married and travelled, then after five years we began to have children. If I had to tell the truth, my story of motherhood has not gone as I would have planned it. At 31-years-old, after about four years of dating, I became a bride for better or for worse; my groom was 39. Neither of us had been married before, nor did we have children. We had simply been enjoying life in our own manner. As newlyweds, we were determined to make marriage work, while acknowledging that being on our own for so long meant some of the natural marital adjustments had to be through deliberate and conscious efforts. We'd even made jokes about making sure at this point in our lives we stayed together, even if staying together meant one person had to take the upstairs portion of the house while the other took the downstairs.

That notion, and a notion of happily ever after, ended with a trip to the hospital emergency room eight years later. I met my husband at the hospital, but I would leave alone. I was shocked, devastated, pregnant, and to top it off, I had a toddler with a critical health issue who would turn three-years-old just a few days afterwards. It would be many months later before it was determined that he had died from sepsis.

And, so my life began as a single mom. I know mothers who chose to be a single mother. That is not my story. Mine is a position in life not chosen by me, but one that was handed to me by God. That was in 2004.

Through it all, I have learned some valuable lessons. I have spoken with mothers who became single mothers through divorce and by choice. In many ways our motherhood joys and challenges are similar. Therefore, while acknowledging that telling my story puts my not-so-pretty life "out there," it is my hope that the words I share for single mothers in the following few pages are helpful to any single mom, regardless of how she came to that status.

## ⏻ Lesson 1: Take time to laugh

I will never forget the day I fully realized I had simply been going through the motions. It came with an innocent declaration from my children: "Mom! You laughed," and then, "Yes, I heard her too." Those simple statements made me cry. Had I really been so preoccupied with making life seem "normal" that I'd forgotten that I loved a good laugh? Had I been so serious and so focused that my children thought it a big deal that I would laugh out loud?

I took a long, hard look at myself then. I recalled one of my son's Mother's Day letters to me. He said he loves all the things I do for him and his brother, and expressed how well I take good care of them ending with, "I can imagine when you were a little girl you enjoyed cooking, cleaning, and working all the time." Yikes! Talk about an eye-opener.

Thankfully, life has changed. The latest Mother's Day letter from one of my sons not only acknowledged how well I take care of them, put a roof over their heads and help them achieve their goals, but said I was doing a fantastic job of it. It went on to say that he appreciates all the "crazy, embarrassing dance moves that I proudly show off" and that "I'm funny, smart, and youthful." Talk about coming a long way from when I first became a single mom. Then, I was solely focused on getting one child delivered here safely and keeping the other one here on earth. Once we got over that hurdle, I became focused on the necessities such as: getting bills paid and homework done, and then remembering to send checks for lunch money and daycare. In reflection, I later saw how even "fun" activities weren't necessarily so fun for my young children. As we'd come in the door from any given sports practice, I would become a robot—sitting one at the table to eat while the other had a bath. Then I'd swap them, and we'd move on to the next activity that needed to be completed before bedtime. I'm sure I'm not the only one who's been in that vicious cycle.

I'd been so caught up in the hectic cycle of life that I'd forgotten to laugh. Even more importantly, I'd forgotten that my precious babies were watching me and possibly taking their signals from me. After that realization, I made it my goal to make sure they saw me in lights other than that of being a mother. For instance, they saw me as a boss—conducting a meeting, or any given training. They also saw me making a speech, or giving a presentation. They saw me as a woman, taking extra care with hair and wearing lipstick, nail polish, and growing my nails out again. They saw me as a community member, having them volunteer alongside me to help others who were more needy than them. Finally, they saw me as a person who lived— dancing, climbing on the monkey bars, or chasing them at the park. They needed to know that I might be Mom, but I was also a mother who could laugh and a mother who could have fun, too. As I like to tell them when they are surprised by something I do, know, or say, "I wasn't always a mommy."

Sometimes we, as busy dedicated mothers, get caught up in this business called life. We go to work; we clean house; we cook; we tend to whatever obligations to which we are committed, and we have our children's best interests at heart, so our focus is solely with them. If the father is not present for whatever reason, this doesn't leave us with a weekend "off" here and there to regroup. Nor, does it leave much time for other family members, friends, or hobbies.

Just as I learned to laugh again, I have learned that we can't take this life, which is already too short, too serious. We need to do all of our daily "chores" and still laugh sometimes. I suggest you laugh just because the kids are laughing, laugh because you dropped and broke the glass, laugh because you got lost trying to get to the doctor's office that you've been to a thousand times before. Just LAUGH. You and your children will feel better for it.

## ⏻ Lesson 2: Take time to smell the roses

Like any mother does in this day and age, I have quite a lot on my plate. I am a serious personality by nature, but I've always liked to have fun, explore new places, and experience different activities. In my pre-motherhood life, I'd scour the calendar sections and travel sections of my local paper as if I had "baller" money. Then, after the internet became more advanced, there I was—with more options— always looking for a new adventure. I still love a bargain.

I had gotten down to nearly 100 pounds and wearing my eight-year-old child's belt in order to keep my pants up, and still didn't realize I had been pushing myself too hard. It took my being physically sick and a kind, but firm, doctor explaining my medical chart—in not so nice layman's terms—that I realized the gravity of what I had done to myself. I was headed toward total physical and mental collapse, from which she couldn't guarantee a quick return. She put it bluntly, "You say you are the only one who is responsible for your children, but someone will have to take over when you find yourself in the hospital!"

That woke me up. I hadn't been smelling the roses. What happened to the person (me) who loved to travel, organize parties, see a good movie, hang out with family and friends, or even cultivate quiet quality time for herself? Life happened, but it shouldn't have happened so harshly. More importantly, it should not have made my innocent children victims as well.

I didn't realize the pressure I was putting on my kids. When I picked them up from daycare, what they heard from me was, "No, I can't let you finish that game," or "No, I don't have time today to see such and such; I'll see it tomorrow. Hurry. We have to go to..." After their sporting events I was saying, "Hurry. We have to get home to get ready..." We'd quickly go through our nighttime routine only to begin again the next day. At night, I'd collapse in bed from exhaustion.

And even with that rush, rush, rush mindset there was no real routine for us. My kids learned to be flexible because they had no choice. We didn't have a set mealtime and rarely adhered to a set bedtime. I had to learn to be flexible as well.

Once I'd physically and mentally healed, I realized what I had been doing to myself. I decided that once a year, no matter what went on, the three of us would take a no agenda vacation, even if it was only a local getaway. That time was ours to do with whatever we pleased. We have taken advantage of our time almost consistently for nearly 10 years, and have not only enjoyed the time together, but have had memorable adventures. During our time, we get up when we want to get up, we might play games, ride horses, kayaks, or go simulated surf boarding. It is not uncommon for us to do something simple like go fishing, rent movies, or watch movies from the pool at a resort at night. We also take in the local culture of wherever we are, primarily because I can't get away from sneaking in an educational lesson. It might be a tour, an exhibit, or a unique museum. During those adventures, we might hang out at the pool all day, or go shopping by way of shuttle, ferry, or subway. It has become our time to do with it as we wish without any obligation to anyone but ourselves. My smelling the roses has also become a time of them learning to smell the roses as well.

Smelling the roses, however, isn't always about the annual trips. We started sitting down to dinner together on a more regular basis, and we go around the table to share our day with each other. We had Friday movie nights on the floor of our family room with an air mattress and maybe pizza and popcorn. When their schedules took our Fridays away, we made it a Sunday family day and would choose a different restaurant after church. Sometimes I'd make arrangements, so we'd even take in a "surprise" trip to a place we hadn't been before, or hadn't visited in a long time. Car and Train Museums, Christmas tree lightings, pumpkin patches, Easter egg hunts, and the like became our new- found time together. Our bonding time, like spontaneity, became critical to me and still is. I understand fundamentally that forming our relationship together before they head off to college and their own busy lives will shape our relationships with each other forever. I take that job seriously and, in that sense, my children come first.

To this day, I absolutely love spending as much time as I can with my sons. It helps keep me in tune with them and helps to keep me balanced. Even though they are now teenagers, I have evidence that they enjoy it too because they often offer up suggestions for time spent.

## ⏻ Lesson #3: Get the fight back

Two years after I became a single mom, I had the audacity to change jobs. I took a leap from an assignment I'd been working on for nearly 12 years to one I knew through advice of trusted mentors was in troubled waters. Everyone, including me, decided I could handle it and make a difference. It was a promotion that put me in much closer proximity to home as my primary purpose at that time was to transfer closer to home to be closer to my children. Until my children began elementary school, they were at a daycare center across the street from my office nearly 30 miles from home in busy downtown Los Angeles. I carpooled with them and could visit them during the day when necessary. This all changed when my oldest went to elementary school. I worried that I wouldn't get to him quickly if something happened. Attending school programs and field trips often meant taking an entire day away from the office, rather than a short period of time away. I needed to be able to do both.

But things aren't always what they seem. At the new job, I found myself sometimes bringing my kids from daycare back to work with me to try to complete an unreasonable workload and managing demands. I found myself spending too much of my vacation time working, or answering my work phone while out of town, even though I was on scheduled leave. As a perfectionist, I was accustomed to doing whatever it took to make my agency succeed, but I was foolish not to realize that nothing I did would be sufficient. I'd been tried by a party unwilling to follow the rules of my organization and found lacking because I insisted on my staff following them. I found myself the target of lies and deceit, and it only served to depress my spirit and make me neglect outside matters that I should have cared more about. I realized afterwards that there were times during that dark period that I was very close to having a nervous breakdown.

I cannot tell you the amount of time and money I have lost by not paying close attention, or following up to important matters. I cannot enumerate the times I just didn't have the energy in me to do what needed to be done outside of work at the time. I don't even want to think about the money I have spent in attorney fees and repeals to right wrongs before I awakened and got my fighting spirit back.

The bottom line is this: If you don't fight for yourself, you can't fight for your children. Who better to advocate for them than you? Who knows them better than you? Who else do they share their concerns, dreams, excitement, and fears with but you? And quite frankly, if it's not you, you should be asking yourself why not.

Although I shielded them when they were younger and there were fights on their behalf with doctors and school districts that they'll never know about, my kids clearly remember my battles with the job, the mortgage company, and their teachers, or schools. Through this they learned that I would always have their backs. They have learned to confide in me and that I'll accept the good, the bad, and the ugly, if they are honest with me. They have learned that the worse thing they could do besides lie to me is to have me blindsided by a teacher's call or a principal's summon. Like me, they have made some bad judgement calls and made some mistakes. But through it all, we have tackled some challenges together. In the process of watching me fight for myself and for them, they have also learned how to advocate for themselves. They have learned to speak up, or to fight back, when needed in order to defend themselves. I am always proud when I see them navigate or negotiate a touchy or difficult situation on their own. I chuckle to myself when they tell me after-the-fact about situations they successfully and skillfully handled.

Our kids learn by watching us, and one thing I've taught mine from an early age when they encounter hurtful situations and they are trying to figure out why someone did something to them is that "not all people are nice." Even though it's in our nature to protect and to nurture, we need to make sure we teach our children the proper way to "fight" before they go out into the world. We need to remember that sometimes giving them tools to fight and to live with others means they may have to be in uncomfortable or unfamiliar (not dangerous) situations. In some situations that bother them, they have to know to perfect their game face and not let others see them sweat. As they get into high schools, colleges, and certainly the workplace exposure to all types of people are inherent, and our children must learn these coping skills in order to know how to get along with all types of people in this world.

## ⏻ Lesson #4: It's okay to get mad sometimes

As I've stated before, I know single mothers who consciously decided to be a single mom, and that is not my story. Tackling motherhood alone never interested me.

Even when married, one of our goals had always been that we had to have the primary responsibility for our children. It was something that both my husband and I placed as a high priority before he passed, and I felt as strongly about after he passed. Having assistance was a blessing, but letting others take over was not an option. As a result, when I was working, I was not a mom who allowed too many extra-curricular activities at one time, or to schedule activities that I could not personally attend or take my children to. In my mind, their first job was that of a student, and mine was that of a mother. My job function was often such that I could schedule meetings and lunch breaks around school performances, school sports games, and field trips. But unfortunately, even if they had nothing scheduled that might mean I'd spend my entire lunch hour buying cleats, preparing team snacks, or trying to find the right colored bow tie. The pace I kept as they got older and more involved in school and outside activities became overwhelming, and I'd get MAD.

I was mad because I thought, *How dare I be left to do it ALL?* As a mom with a partner, responsibilities are shared, whether they are formally defined or not. When there's only one caretaker, the burden (yes, burden) of every bill, every game, every doctor or dentist appointment, every school meeting, every battle, and every clean up falls to that one person.

Honestly, there were plenty of times when I'd get outright mad about the situation, I found myself in. Yet, I was not inclined to tell my kids they couldn't participate in any school or community activities because mommy had to work or was too tired. More often than not, I was mad because I was still trying to smile when I was so very tired or equally frustrated that I couldn't think straight.

I also got mad when I found myself lacking. You know the saying, "We are most critical of ourselves." I used to enjoy remembering and acknowledging others' birthdays, special holidays, or special occasions, and I got to the point that I couldn't (still can't sometimes) remember anything. After more than a dozen years as a single mother, I am just now getting to the point where I actually remember to give (or send) cards I'd bought or can locate gifts I'd purchased for others. At my worse, even if I could locate it, it might be delivered in the store bag. School and sports pictures have been purchased and forgotten about, so they remain in a keepsake box. There are people I miss and think about often whom I rarely get to call. In addition to becoming the queen of buying cards and even gifts that I'd misplace or even forget to send, I'd plan for an activity or an outing and forget about it until it was too late. I'd start projects and get called away, never to return to complete them. It literally took years for me to believe I cannot do it all and even longer before I finally got to the point that I can forgive myself for my own shortcomings.

Other things get me angry as well. There are times when I wish life remained some semblance of the same—not just with my husband's death, but life in general. There are times when I'd wonder why I was dealt such a hand. A death, a friend's divorce, even someone else's job changes still mentally throw me off for a period of time. But only those who know me very, very well know this about me because I'd become a master at hiding my feelings and therefore my anger. The real lesson here: It's okay to get mad at life. Just don't unpack, get comfortable, or stay there.

⏻ **Lesson #5: Do the things you don't feel like doing.**

I will forever treasure a bit of advice I received from one of my best girlfriends early in my single motherhood journey. She said, "If I have one piece of advice for you, it would be to continue going to church even when you don't feel like going." She'd found that bit of advice helpful herself with the death of her sister. When she said that to me, I immediately remembered my mother telling my brother and me in high school, "Don't ditch class. If you go, even if you think you aren't listening, something is bound to stick with you that you will need someday." My relationship with Christ has always been important to me, so I took my friend's words to heart.

There were days when I barely made it to church with a double stroller. There were days when we went to my parents' church primarily, so I could have assistance handling my small children. There were days I'd swear I only heard one word or remembered a song, but we had made it to the house of the Lord that day (any given day).

Church is but one example of how to keep going when you don't feel like it. Often times, as a single mother, you may find yourself happy to simply lay across your bed with the television remote or a good book. It's important, however, to engage sometimes in activities that we don't feel like doing because it keeps us from becoming comfortably isolated. Being isolated from your friends and family, or isolated from the familiar, is not a good place for anyone. As a single mother, however, it can be damaging to our psyche. Isolation can become our "happy place" where we never have to deal with uncomfortable questions. Therefore, we never get past uncomfortable situations.

Doing what you don't feel like doing, especially when it comes to our children, is equally important. After my children realized I could actually laugh, they also learned I could throw and catch a baseball, I could run very fast, that I wasn't just making them learn to swim but that I knew how, and that I knew how to sneak into a movie theater to see a second show if I wanted to. Did I feel like doing those things? Sometimes, I did not. I'd much rather watch them in action while I spent a few precious moments with a book in front of my face, a tablet in hand playing a word game, or the phone up to my ear catching up with a friend.

Conversely, while I believe you should intentionally engage in activities, don't be afraid to stay away from activities you really don't want to do. There were times when I'd talked myself into going to a function when I really didn't want to go. I'd go to support because I thought I should, or simply because I was asked, but my discontent was visible or verbal. I'd tell myself I should continue with tradition or support someone when it only resulted in a disastrous outcome. Change tends to alter our perspective on life. Make it for the better. Choose wisely what you will do and even who you will do it with.

## ⏻ Lesson 6: Don't apologize for being you.

There will always be those people who remember the person you were at the worst point in your life—forgetful, scatterbrained, a little unorganized, half put together, and/or chronically late. In any situation, regardless of the progress you make and how soon you make it, those people will never let you forget it. Those are the same people who conveniently forget that your life, even single life, used to be put much better together. The sad part is that the people I am describing are people who are often very close to you. And even sadder is the fact that those are the ones who attack rather than seek to assist, shield, or understand you.

What they don't know is that overcoming our worse self often takes years—not days or weeks—to accomplish. There are still some things I am working to get past. I have never shared this, but only I knew the days that getting up, getting dressed, and keeping sane through the day was a huge accomplishment. Only I knew the naps I could sneak off and get while I should have been mingling at a family gathering were cherished moments. Only I knew that sometimes I would find myself so needy for adult conversations that I'd have to make conscious efforts not to overkill. Only a few know that I'd busy myself with helping at functions, just so I could avoid interacting on a particularly bad day. Those same few also knew that the smile they saw was often but a façade.

So sometimes, more often than not, a sharp tone or not so nice sentiment would escape from my lips. As I've navigated this business of single motherhood, I have certainly made some mistakes. I have been harsh with others, including my children, and in trying to cope with being a single mother, I have at times been distant to everyone. I have had doubts, some fears, and many tears but continuing with a prosperous life for me and my children has always been my goal.

For the longest time, I didn't have it in me to take the lead in traditions anymore because it took too much out of me. Sometimes, I still do not. When there were two of us working as a team the planning, purchasing, executing, and aftermath of an event was a shared responsibility. It felt less like work and more like fun. When that changed, I realized some people had no regard for my new normal. I simply could not do everything I used to do and do it with the same quality, especially when my children were very young.

A good friend of mine, whom I have lost touch with, pointed out to me once that I tended to apologize when apologies weren't necessary. I'd say, "Yes, I got my master's degree because..." "I have a house, but..." I didn't realize the significance of that statement until I became a single mother, and it seemed like I was always apologizing. I had to learn not to apologize after I had done my best and still fallen short. I had to learn also to quietly forgive those who only chose to remember the worse in me while forgetting that at one time I was a better person to them. When I can't forgive and still remain in touch, I have quietly cut people loose. Probably most important was I had to learn that no one is owed an explanation or apology for me being a widow/single mother. Life happens.

I also had to learn when to apologize and when not to apologize to my children. Like many of us, I have encountered moments when one of my children declares me the "most horrible mother in the world." Worse, there have been times when I have felt like the worse mother in the world. I will not apologize for doing my best. I have never been the mom who missed many school events or games, and I even volunteer on a regular basis and held positions on school committee and boards—then and now. However, I might doze off during their favorite television show, or come late to pick up from practice because I was trying to complete that one last errand. I might even wait too late to purchase the concert tickets I'd promised and have to come up with a viable substitute.

If what you do as a mother isn't harmful or malicious, in the end it's okay. We can only do what we know to be best at the time. As a single parent, we sometimes have to make decisions off the cuff with no one to bounce them off of. Apologize to your children, others, and yourself for mistakes, missteps, and even the occasional unkindness but never apologize for being you. Do not compromise your values for the comfort of others. My parents were a little strict, so I may have been a different, somewhat sheltered child in some ways, but my parents didn't do too shabby with me and my brother.

I know I don't have the patience I used to have, but through this journey of single motherhood, I have grown thicker skin in some ways; and my skin has become thinner in others, but my intentions are always good. People may not always understand or agree with my actions, but I never apologize for doing what I believe to be in the best interest for my children and myself.

## ⏻ Lesson 7: Your quality of life is important (too)

As a newly single mom, I tried to keep all the balls afloat. Reality took a long time to set in for me because the shock of all that had happened to me in such a short period of time still sticks with me in ways. After all, I had plans. I had short and long-term goals. The next few years were all laid out.

I'd never had a problem spending time with myself doing activities I love, having a dinner or drinks, taking in the local entertainment, or even taking solo weekend travel getaways. In order for me to be the best for myself and my children, I needed to continue doing those things, but I must confess that I let myself get away from taking care of me. I was 109 pounds with my hair falling out by the comb full before I realized I wasn't taking care of me. Yet, I kept pushing. After all, I had to do it all myself didn't I? I would have loved to save the money I pay for a housekeeper and handymen but having those "luxuries" meant more discretionary free time for my household. It meant I didn't spend all of my days off or weekends cleaning and running errands... and getting mad about it.

Thankfully, by the time my youngest entered elementary school, I remembered that taking time for myself didn't take away from them. I realized that it would've been different if all I did for myself was without them. I am not a mother where I never include or even consider them. *Quite the opposite.* As they got older, however, I learned when to incorporate them into family friendly activities and when to leave them to their own devices. Even now, they might ask me, "Who did you go with?" But they are never surprised when I respond, "No one," or "By myself."    In that respect, they are comfortable doing the same. And as an aside, they never have a doubt that I make time to support at whatever they undertake.

If I leave you with nothing else, it is with the reminder that while you endeavor to spend time with your friends and family, make sure to carve out time to spend with yourself too. Your physical and mental health are important. This was the hardest lesson for me to learn.

## ⏻ Lesson #8: Don't disregard your village

I only have one sibling, but my extended family is huge. I learned to know who would genuinely assist me in a bind and who would always have a reason why they could not. I learned to recognize who only looked out for themselves and who would help me make it happen. This is important to me still because not only did it teach me who I could rely on, but I made sure those individuals knew they can rely on me as well. It has to go both ways. This was critical to me because I cannot tell you the number of times I asked someone if they could pick up or drop off my kids because I was in a tight situation, and their getting back to me never happened; or, they needed to see if someone else could do it instead. As an independent personality by nature, I have always tried to do it all myself. If I found myself in a position to ask for anything from anyone that meant I really, really needed the help and had exhausted all other options.

My parents have been the biggest part of my village, but they are not my sole village. I am forever grateful that they took on a role they thought they had outgrown by stepping in to help in so many ways when I found myself a widow and a single parent. Not all empty-nesters would have been able or willing.

I will tell any mother, whether single or not, to cultivate your village. I am blessed to have had my parents, some family members (including a few in-laws), and my closest friends in my circle as my support group. I absolutely TREASURE my village.

Everyone needs to have a friend who will leave her own small children to fly cross country to be with you to help you with your newborn when your toddler has his last of a series of heart surgeries. That's the same friend who wouldn't change her plans when the surgery was postponed for a few months simply because she felt she needed to do a barometer check on me. Everyone needs to have that friend who will jump on a plane in a time of crisis and get to your kitchen, cooking dinner for a houseful of mourners when you walk in your home. While she did this, she had her husband outside mowing the grass and tidying the yard. Everyone needs to have that sister-cousin who will pray with you, as well as for you and your children, who will advocate on your behalf when you don't even know they are doing so. Everyone needs a relative who doesn't have children, by choice, but will come to spend a week or two chauffeuring their nephews around, so they wouldn't have to get up at the crack of dawn in the summer because mommy had to work and summers were crunch-time for her. Everyone needs to have a family friend who will schedule herself to go with my mother several times a week to take my son to the lab. She would distract him, feed him, and comfort him several times a week for months. Yes, those friends/family are part of my village.

I also have an awesome group of mom-friends who've been meeting monthly for a dozen years. We have laughed, cried, shared confidences, and even argued sometimes. We started out volunteering at our children's school together and, even though our children are at different schools and different grade levels now, we still meet and sometimes share special occasions. Some of the oldest kids in the group are now in college; yet, we have continued our ability to talk about most everything when we get together—from school accomplishments and pitfalls, to social media, rumors, testing, and anything the kids are talking about and concerned about. There are times now we can't always meet together as regularly as a full group, but our regular meeting date continues with a few or all of us. We also have impromptu meet ups. Regardless of how many or how often we gather together, I'd like to think that the close relationship is still there.

My village includes sets of male individuals who cater to my sons. My youthful father has been a constant in my sons' lives and has imparted into them in ways that only a seasoned, distinguished, and wise man could. There are also a few very trusted males who were great friends of my late husband who have taken it upon themselves to reach out to my kids, to interject themselves into my two boys' lives, and to speak wisdom to them as their father would. In the case of one dear friend who lives and works quite a distance away, he has always made it a point to show up at important events at least once a season. I am forever grateful because they have all provided a male perspective that I cannot.

I am okay with people who don't think the same as I do sharing their opinion with my children. My children aren't followers and have strong minds. I think it's healthy, and it gives them a different perspective to sort through. When they try to sort through an adult's opinion that might be different from theirs, we discuss it. I speak with my children about how and why the person may see it differently and has a different perspective. Now in their teens, I know some of what they hear will be the same as what I've said but will be received differently primarily because it didn't come from me. I also realize that the life experiences of others may cause them to see matters in a different light, and that perspective is not necessarily wrong. In fact, I believe it's good for my children to consider them. When they head off to college and get jobs, they will encounter all types of individuals from all kinds of backgrounds, and it is my goal that they know how to co-exist with them, as well handle them without compromising themselves.

As a single mother you may not realize the value or the power of your village, or you may think you do not have one. If you find that you truly don't have a support group, you need to prayerfully cultivate one. My village continues to amaze me, and with my village I also know—without being told—that my children and I are covered by some in prayer and by love.

## ⏻ Lesson 9: FINALLY, Dare to Dream again (and always pray).

Saying dare to dream again sounds so cliché, but it is such an important facet of life. I had always said that the advantage of having kids later in life meant I would have a lot of work years under my belt already and could retire while they were still young. It was my goal to get to that magical place in my company's hierarchy and walk away to a new, less demanding, or a better part-time gig.

I stopped thinking about those dreams when I became a single parent because I thought they were no longer achievable. It took me a very long while to realize otherwise. When I reached the point in my life where I was thinking "my husband died when I was this age, my mom died ten years later, and in another ten years both my kids would have finished high school and/or college and started a different life path" and citing it like a daily mantra in my head, I knew it was time to retire. It was like I had suddenly remembered there was more to life than what I was doing. I had a house I wanted to enjoy more; I had children I wanted to nurture more; and, I still had dreams I was young enough to pursue and talents I wanted to explore.

Although I literally walked into my office on Tuesday and told them that Thursday of the same week would be my last day in the office, I'd already made final preparations beginning months and months in advance. As always, I was the planner and the optimist.

My retirement paperwork had been completed about six months before I'd begun making annual treks to the retirement board years before. I had done financial charts after financial charts and checked into every possible nuance to determine if my plan would work. Most of all, I had convinced myself that anything would be better than the hectic pace that was slowly killing me.

I had enough years working at that particular job to get a decent salary and very good benefits. I had learned the hard way that you can't take it with you. The way I saw it there was literally nothing holding me back, since I was still young enough to work elsewhere, preferably part-time, so I'd have time to pursue the dreams I had been keeping in the back of my head. I took the leap. It was scary, but I've never looked back—even though some adjustments had to be made because my finances have taken a huge hit. That circumstance creates a fear for a money manager like me.

I fully understand that it is quite difficult to dream again when it seems everything your hand touches literally falls apart, and every business and personal matter that should be simple isn't. I understand that from personal experience. I also know the dreams I had for myself and my children, and I am determined to see them through. They are good, well-rounded, normal boys.

As luck would have it, life has dealt us some pretty big successes and some pretty hard challenges. Together my children and I have experienced hurts and pitfalls, but we do so *together*—beginning with when I prayed for them while they were in my womb. I still pray for them today. But also together, my children and I have enjoyed life and each other. We have come to understand each other. I listen to their adventures and hear them engage with others and am proud of the relationships they've developed and the qualities they exhibit. They have so much potential. I am sure that like me in my youth, my kids have lied to save face with their peers at times. It's wrong, but it's harmless.

Your dreams my not be my dreams, but if you think you have to let go of your dreams because you are a single mom, think again, then dare to dream again.

I wish I could share that I have the magic combination but, after 14 years of single motherhood, I still do not. Like any parent raising children, single or not, there is a lot of trial and error. What works for one child, doesn't work for another. I have inadvertently given my heart healthy baby his heart warrior brother's medication. We have had breakfast for dinner and dinner for breakfast more times than I'd like to share. I know this if I know nothing else, my boys will be just fine with whatever life throws their way. I am looking forward to seeing and experiencing all that God has in store for us. I am absolutely loving this season of our lives. My life as a mother hasn't gone as I would have scripted it, and I've had to learn some tough life lessons along the way, but there is little I would change.

## Where do you find your POWER?

My power lies in my identity. I became unstoppable once I realized I am not what has happened to me. I am not my mistakes, and I am more than a woman with a sad story; rather, I am who God says I am.

# CHAPTER 6

## ABUSED BUT NOT BROKEN

### By Keshia Roberts

---

I remember it like it was yesterday. It was Christmas Day at Catholic Charities Residential Treatment Center, which is just a really fancy name for orphanage. I was six years old. My group and I were the youngest at the orphanage, and we called ourselves "The Violets." Several weeks prior, everyone was instructed to write down three gifts we wanted for Christmas. The lists were sent off to be put on The Angel Tree. I, being the inexperienced orphan, was very unfamiliar with this process. I was told I could put anything I wanted! So, that is exactly what I did. I dreamed big... a little too big.

I put some very expensive gifts on my list and ended up receiving only a coloring book and a VHS of a bible story on Christmas Day. I was disappointed to say the least. However, a member of my group was lucky enough to receive a Magic Eight Ball. I, and the rest of "The Violets," sat in the hallway and took turns eagerly asking the eight ball questions, shook the ball vigorously, and waited for its prediction. The questions my groupmates asked were fairly innocent, seemingly normal six-year-old questions. But my curiosity ran deeper than the norm. When it was my turn with the ball I asked if I would ever get married. I was immediately reprimanded by the staff who was monitoring our group at the time. I was told that I was too young to be asking questions about boys, and before the eight ball could answer it was taken from me and passed to the next girl. Confused and frustrated, I waited for the ball to come back around to me. This time I did not ask about a boy or a relationship. Rather, I asked if I would ever have children. Once again I was reprimanded, but this time I wasn't allowed to play again. So before the ball could answer I was sent to the room that was assigned to us and instructed to color in the book I was gifted.

This is my first recollection of my burning desire to have a family of my own. I'm not quite sure how, or why, I possessed this desire, since almost every example of family I had up until that point in my life was dysfunctional and abusive to say the very least. My biological mother was a heroin addict and a prostitute who struggled to care for myself and my siblings. When I was one year old, she asked the neighbor to babysit me while she went to the store, and she never came back. The neighbors cared for me for about a month with the hopes that my mother would return. She never did. So, they were forced to call Child Protective Services.

From there I was placed in my first foster home, the Greeve family. They were a wonderful family; however, the parents were up in age and not looking to permanently adopt any children. Child Protective Services assured them that because I was so young, they would be able to place me with a family member in no time. However, it proved to be more difficult than they expected. Because of the strained relationships between my mother and the rest of the family, no one agreed to take me in. My own father even refused and permanently signed away his parental rights. This process ended up lasting three years. Three, very long, critical years of my life. At the age of four CPS was able to find an adoptive family for me and I was ripped, literally ripped, from my home. I remember kicking, screaming, crying, and clinging onto every piece of furniture I could wrap my little hands around as my new adoptive parents and caseworker drug me out of the house.

The Lipinski family was all set to adopt me. The entire ride to my new home they tried to explain to my four-year-old mind that this was the best placement for me because I was bi-racial, and they were an interracial couple. However, I did not understand race. All I wanted was to go home. Back to the only home and the only family I had ever known. About a week after I was settled into the Lipinski household, the abuse started. My adoptive mother-to-be worked full-time, and my adoptive father and brother-to-be were home with me most of the day. Every day she left for work, I was abused sexually. I was only four-years-old, and here were these men who had uprooted me from everything I knew and promised to take care of me, yet I was made into their sex slave, literally. I became so angry... *so very angry*. I started fighting back, which led to other abuse. If I didn't comply, I was whipped and locked in either my room closet or the garage and denied food. All of this took place only while my mother was at work. I never told her what was going on; I was too afraid.

After about a year, I eventually told a neighbor who immediately called Child Protective Services, and I was removed from their home the very next day. From there I was placed with the Peterson family. This family had agreed to adopt me as well, but they were also abusive. At this point, I was too angry to comply with any abuse or mistreatment. I began fighting. Every time I felt I was being treated differently, I fought. Life turned into a battle of the wills. My will vs. the will of my adoptive mother. This is where I learned that, in life, I would have to fend for myself. I was actually adopted by the Petersons, and my name was changed from Keshia La'Vet Moore to Keshia Alexandria Peterson. But the adoption did not last long.

I continued fighting until eventually I was placed in a psychiatric facility when I was only six-years-old. I remember walking down a hall to my assigned padded room. Along the way there were people in straight-jackets yelling and screaming through the tiny windows on every door. I was terrified. After a weeklong stay there, I was taken to Catholic Charities. The Petersons reversed my adoption, and I never saw them again.

Despite every life event up until that point, I longed for a healthy family of my own. I would imagine having children who looked like me. I told myself I would be better to my kids than my mother and foster mothers had been to me. I would imagine holiday traditions I could start with my family. I wanted it so badly. I recall being very embarrassed whenever anyone would ask me what I wanted to be when I grew up. While other kids would ramble off professions, such as a doctor or teacher or police officer, the only thing I could think of was a mother. The reactions I would get were hardly ever positive. I was repeatedly told that I should have higher aspirations for myself. It just seemed like no one understood me. Eventually, I began telling anyone who asked that I aspired to be a lawyer. The reactions were so much better... "Ah, yes!" "You'll make a great attorney!" "You'll make so much money!" But, deep down inside, all I wanted was to be a wife and a mother.

After about a year and a half stay at Catholic Charities, I was placed with yet another foster family, The Murphy's. The Murphy's were different than any other foster family I had lived with in the past. I was their very first foster child. While they were optimistic and eager to love and care for me, I was apprehensive and abrasive. I just did not trust anyone. The Murphy's did everything they could to provide me with a good quality of life: I attended private school, I was involved in extra-curricular activities, I was able to attend acting classes, and I was given birthday parties. I remember having the best Christmas of my life at their house. They really were amazing. I remember, particularly, the love I received from Mr. Murphy. He would always compliment me. He was constantly telling me I was beautiful and talented. Anything I was interested in doing, they allowed me to try. But, I was still angry. In spite of everything they did for me, I terrorized their home. I threw tantrum after tantrum. I just did not know how to receive their love.

Eventually, I was asked to leave their home and was placed in the home of Mrs. Roberts. She was the school computer teacher I had while I lived at Catholic Charities. During the time I attended her school, she always treated me like a daughter. It was hard being an orphan and getting dropped off by the "orphan van" at school. Kids quickly began to make fun of me. They would make fun of my off-brand shoes and my limited wardrobe. They laughed at my frizzy and unruly hair. They also made fun of the fact that I didn't have a family. That is what hurt me most. Unbeknownst to me, Mrs. Roberts was actually a foster parent for the same agency I lived with. She quickly swooped in and became my "school mama." She would allow me to come to her classroom in the mornings instead of waiting in the gym, which is where most of the taunting took place. She kept a bucket of bows and every morning she would always comb my hair really cute. She would sign papers that needed parent signatures for me, and every day she would give me a quarter for lunch, so that I could buy a snack. It was such a surreal experience to actually be living in her home. The Roberts were experienced foster parents. My tantrums hardly affected them. I lived with them for roughly three years, and at the age of eleven I was adopted by them and they became my actual forever family. My name was now officially Keshia Denise Roberts.

From that point on, I lived a normal adolescent life. I was a popular girl in school. I had a lot of friends. I was captain of the varsity cheerleading squad. I seemed to be the poster child for happiness. Whenever I would open up about my childhood, my friends would be shocked. I seemed so happy, and my life appeared so perfect, that my actual past was hard for people to believe. In actuality I was happy, but deep down I felt empty. Even though I had an adoptive family that loved me, I wanted a family of my own. After high school I watched my friends, one by one, go off to college and embark on their own life journeys. While they pursued college and careers, the only dream I had was still to be a wife and a mother.

Eventually I attended community college, so that I could "look normal." But I never picked a major. I just aimlessly enrolled in the collegiate basics. I had always been smart, so I excelled in every class I took, but I was still empty. Two summers after I graduated high school, I began working at a summer camp for the YMCA. It was there that I met and fell in love with Calvin. We were inseparable. We worked together; we went to school together; we did everything together. I just knew this was going to be the person I was going to spend the rest of my life with. After two years of dating, our relationship started to change. He had finished his courses at the community college we both attended and enrolled in a four-year university about an hour away from where we lived. While he was looking to pursue his dream career, I was still clinging to my dream. So, of course, I did everything I could to support him. I remember staying up all night writing essays for him. I remember giving him answers for entrance exams he was having difficulty passing. I did everything I could. I was operating like I was already his wife. Which, in my mind, was what I was supposed to do if I ever wanted to actually get married. That was a huge mistake. I wanted so badly for things to go as I had planned them in my mind ever since I was a child that I never saw I was actually being manipulative.

Needless to say, once he went away to college our relationship took a drastic turn. The visits home slowly decreased. The calls became shorter and contained less and less substance. Deep down I knew it was over between us, but by this point I was 23 years old and felt like my dreams were slipping away. It's almost comical to me now when I realize that I was so young and had so many real opportunities in front of me. But, in my mind, I was behind. In my mind, I was supposed to be married with a house and a dog… and a child… with another one on the way. In my mind, it was too late to start over with anyone else. So, I stayed. Even after I knew I was being cheated on, I stayed. I stayed until I eventually became pregnant. This was by far the most shame I had ever experienced in my life.

Never in my wildest dreams did I imagine I would become a

mother without first becoming a wife. Calvin and I contemplated abortion, but in our hearts, we knew we could never go through with it. A few months into my pregnancy, we decided to officially break up. I was devastated. I had no clue what I was going to do. The way I coped with everything was to ignore it. Despite my growing belly, I ignored it. I did not even seek prenatal care until the end of my second trimester. I had not bought a single diaper, wipes, crib, nothing. The truth is I really couldn't afford to buy anything. I worked a minimum wage job and made enough to get by as a single woman, but nothing more.

I remember the night my pregnancy finally became real to me. I was lying in bed, and I saw my baby flip over in my stomach. I couldn't believe it. It was amazing and terrifying at the same time. That night I laid in my bed and told myself I was going to end up being just like my birth mother. A woman who couldn't take care of her kids. That thought alone broke my heart. Eventually, I told Calvin we had to start getting serious about the baby and find a doctor and start making arrangements. That is when the accusations started. He told me he did not believe the child belonged to him, since he had been away to school. That literally broke my heart. Looking back at it now, I can say the accusation derived from fear. He was just as afraid as I was. Even so, it was painful. Despite all the accusations, procrastination, and shame, I gave birth to a healthy baby boy.

Calvin Crosby, V was born on September 10, 2011, weighing in at eight pounds and six ounces and measuring 21" long. He was everything I thought he would be and more. However, the joy of birth was quickly interrupted by the dysfunction of my on-and-off-again, off again, relationship with Calvin. I stayed in the hospital for three days because my blood pressure was through the roof. Each day I had the occasional visitor, but for the most part I was alone. A feeling I knew all too well.

The first year of motherhood was very stressful and unstable. I eventually lost my job and had absolutely no income. I had lost my apartment and was living with my son's grandparents. They did the best they could to accommodate me and their grandson, but it was never a comfortable living situation to me. Mostly because it was not the life I had in my mind for my son and me. On the outside I was the doting mother with the handsome new baby boy. I seemed to be able to provide the best of everything for him, but my whole entire life was a mirage. The reality was I was broke, depressed, and alone. I remember nights where baby Calvin would be relentlessly crying. It seemed like nothing I did would soothe him. I remember thinking to myself, *This is why God designed for you to be married before you have children because raising a baby is truly a two-person job.* I also remember thinking, *I understand, now, how some women snap and shake their baby!* Despite all the frustration, I pressed on and Calvin continued to grow happy and healthy.

Shortly after his first birthday, Baby Calvin and I moved to live with his father. We decided to give our relationship another chance for the sake of our child. It was an idea based solely out of desperation and probably the worst idea we ever had. We knew there was no romantic love between us, yet we tried. We continued to display the image of a happy and healthy family. While deep down we were slowly growing to hate one another. Every day I was happy to see him leave to go to class, and I'm sure he was just as happy to leave. I remember one night when Calvin came in and sat on the edge of the bed and said, "For the first time ever, I actually don't think we are going to make it." Deep down inside I agreed, but I didn't show it. I walked outside for hours in the middle of the night. I sat down on an electrical box and cried until tears could no longer stream down my face. So many thoughts filled my head. I began to feel so sorry for myself. I blamed everything and everyone except myself for where I was in life. I told myself that if my mom would have just taken care of me like she was supposed to, then I would have never been in this situation. I convinced myself that I would never be able to take care of my son on my own. I was so sure that no man would ever want me now that I had a child. I had no idea what I was going to do, or where I was going to go now that I was single. I had no job and no money. In retrospect, I think the thing that was damaged the most was my pride. How in the world was I supposed to portray that I had a happy and healthy family now that we were broken up for good?

I sat outside in the dark, and these thoughts and more clouded my mind and my judgement. It all became too much. I got up and walked back to the apartment. I went to the bathroom and found a bottle of pain killers I was prescribed after I gave birth. One by one, I consumed the whole bottle. Right there with my precious baby asleep on the bed, I attempted to take my life. In the moments while I was taking the pills, I was convinced that I was ready to die. I had convinced myself that Baby Calvin would be better off without me because I was not able to provide for him anyway. I knew that his dad and grandparents would step up and raise him if they had no other choice. Then, as I felt the last of the pills sliding down my throat something switched. I started imagining all the people who loved me and how devastated they would be when they found out I had taken my own life. I imagined Baby Calvin starting school without me and playing sports without me there to cheer him on. I imagined him having to explain to people that his mother killed herself when he was a baby. I could almost feel his pain because it was the same pain I felt having to explain that my mother gave me away when I was baby. I remember sitting on the bed essentially waiting to die. I kept throwing up over and over. I was so sick and dizzy, I could barely stand. It was in that moment that I felt God speak to me. He said so clearly, "I'll change your situation, if you let Me change your heart." I remember being very confused. *Change my heart?* At that time I didn't see anything wrong with me, mostly because I never took the time to look. Eventually I started praying, which is something I had only done in church. I prayed to God that He would keep me alive if He was real. I prayed and apologized. I apologized for trying to take my life after Jesus gave up His for me. I apologized for trying to make things happen on my own. I promised God that I would live for Him, and that was pretty much all I knew to say.

This was the most pivotal moment of my life. In an apartment with a belly full of pills, I received salvation. I was literally hours away from death, yet God gave me life because I chose Him. I stayed up that whole night because I was afraid that if I fell asleep, I wouldn't wake up. And by the morning I felt totally fine. Calvin and I had a conversation about what Baby Calvin and I were supposed to do since I had no job, no money, and no place to go. He suggested I try and find a women's shelter that would take us in. I was so offended. It was in that moment when I knew we had absolutely no chance of reconciling, and I truly had to figure this out on my own. I was able to reach out to my best friend, and she agreed to let me come stay with her. That was hard for me to do because it required vulnerability. I had to destroy the image I portrayed to everyone and admit that I actually had nothing and desperately needed her help. I waited for Calvin to leave for class, and I packed up my stuff.

Every single thing I owned fit in two suitcases and a tote. I put it in my car, and I left. Despite everything that had taken place in the last 24 hours, I had an overwhelming sense of peace that I knew could only come from God. I encouraged myself the whole drive back home. I promised myself that I would hold it together for my son. I told myself that I was done feeling sorry for myself, and I wasn't going to let my son see me depressed and defeated. I promised myself that I would not become bitter. The following Sunday, I visited a church that had just opened in my hometown two months prior and fell in love with it. The worship was everything I needed. The teaching was like nothing I had ever heard before. It was actually interesting, and I could actually relate to it. Eventually, I joined and began serving in ministry. I had so much hope and faith that my life would turn around for the better. And it did, eventually. The process, however, was taxing—to say the least. My naivety made me believe now that I was living right and going to church, doors were supposed to start opening. I really believed that things were supposed to start magically happening. I didn't understand there would be a process that came along with it.

As I grew closer to God and learned more about Him, I subsequently learned more about myself, and that was hard. There were many things I realized I did not like about myself at all. It was hard to realize I had tendencies and proclivities that were ugly, hurtful, and manipulative. It was painful to realize that even though I was a victim for many years, I was not completely innocent. I accepted the fact that there were so many opportunities I'd let slip out of my hands due to fear and procrastination. In a way I had crippled myself, and I was now dealing with the fruits of those bad decisions. I began dealing with those things, day by day. It was not easy, but my faith helped me hold everything together.

After three months, my son and I were able to move into an apartment of our own. By this point his father had started to reach out to visit him, which helped me a lot. I did not have much at all. The only furniture my apartment had was a twin bed and a dresser. I worked a job as a caterer, so I was able to eat at work and bring leftovers home for dinner. A family friend who had a set of twins a year older than Calvin passed down clothes and shoes to us every season. And, day by day, we made it. We continued to make it until I eventually got a better job paying three times what I was making as a caterer. I was making more than I had ever made in my life, and it felt amazing. I remember how good it felt to finally shop for my son and buy him clothes that I wanted for him. I remember the first time I was able to put gifts under a Christmas tree for him. I remember being able to give him a room with his own bed and his own toys. It meant so much to do all the little things people can so easily take for granted. And, still today, I hold these things dear because I know what it is not to be able to do them.

For single mothers, it can be so easy to become bitter instead of making a decision to become better. I understand that no two people in life are awarded the same opportunities. Because of this, it's so easy to make excuses for yourself. But the reality is that your past does not have to dictate your future. I've spoken to so many young mothers who think that because they weren't given a healthy example of motherhood, marriage, or family that they will never be able to have one. That is simply not the truth. If every example of family you were given was dysfunctional, take that and don't repeat it! It's a simple process of elimination. If your mother was hurtful, don't do what she did. Surround yourself with positive influences. Read books and watch videos on how to better yourself—for yourself and your children. The tools and strategies are available if we would just open our hearts and minds to them.

We also have to make a conscience decision that everything we do will be in the best interest of our children. I told myself I would never deny my son's father the opportunity to spend time with his child. I did not care how upset I was for the way he treated me because that had nothing to do with the way he feels about his son. Just because our relationship did not last, does not mean he doesn't deserve to have one with his child. In a way, foster care prepared me to deal with co-parenting because I knew what it felt like to live without my parents. I never wanted my son to have to feel that. I surely would never be able to live with myself if I knew his father wanted a relationship, and I was getting in the way. This perspective has made co-parenting for us very easy. Calvin's father has since gotten married and started a family of his own. He spends just about as much time with Calvin as I do. He shows up to Calvin's activities with his family, and we all support my son. He loves all of us, and I wouldn't have it any other way.

And lastly, I want every single mother reading this to know there is hope. Being single and raising children is not a death sentence. You can still have the quality of life you've always dreamed of. You can still have the marriage, the family, the house, the dog, and the picket fence; it will just require discipline and strategy. If you spend time focusing your mind on the positive things you desire and how you can achieve them, you will be surprised how things start to shift for you. It is easy to dwell on what went wrong, who left you, who was never there for you, the list goes on and on. But that kind of thinking will never propel you forward. Your children need a "healthy you" if you plan on raising them effectively. This means healthy physically, emotionally, and spiritually. Figure out what you want out of life for you and your children, and formulate a plan.

The most effective way to move forward is to realistically evaluate and accept where you are. Think about a map. The first thing you search for is the marker that says, "you are here." Without that, it doesn't matter where you want to go; you'll never be able to get there if you first don't know where you are. Accepting where you are is sometimes the hardest part because it can be disappointing and even embarrassing, but it's necessary. The encouraging part is, once you realize where you are, you don't have to stay there. Jesus tells us in John 8:32, "And ye shall know the truth, and the truth shall make you free." (KJV) Bishop T.D. Jakes expounded on that simple verse in a way that changed my life. He said, "The reason you feel stuck is because your story is not your truth. It is simply the story you have told yourself. Because, if it were the truth, it would have set you free." I will carry that concept with me for the rest of my life, and I implore you to do the same. Evaluate yourself and your situation, and if the outcome doesn't free you, then it's not the truth. Sometimes you may have to dig deeper—deeper inside your heart, deeper inside your insecurities, and even deeper into your short comings. But the truth is somewhere! And guess what, when you find that truth, it's going to MAKE you free! It's not going to open a gate and set you free; rather, it is going to literally propel you forward whether you want to go or not. So, continue to put one foot in front of the other. Your children are watching, and they're following. Blazing the trail for them alone is not easy, but it is possible. Before you realize it, you'll be walking into things you never imagined before. You're not the first single mother, and you won't be the last. Be encouraged. Your children are depending on you.

# ABOUT THE AUTHORS

## Chassity Heard

Chassity Heard, BSCLS, MHA is a 32 year old Houston native, and a proud mother to her adorable daughter. She has been working in the healthcare field since 2008. She was featured in the "Women of Distinction" magazine for her career accomplishments in the healthcare field. Chassity is using her years of expertise to pour into students pursuing their bachelor's degree in Healthcare Administration as an Adjunct Professor at Belhaven University. While balancing her career in healthcare and motherhood Chassity coaches' middle school and high school student athletes. Her mission is to empower teen girls and young women to overcome their fear of not being enough, and to help them embrace their God-given identity and purpose. In 2016, Chassity helped develop a single mother's ministry called M.O.M.S. Den, or Mothers On a Mission to Succeed. In 2016, she turned her love for brownies into a business called "The Brownie Spot".

## Sylvia Thomas

Sylvia Grady Phillips is a native of San Antonio, Texas. She has lived in Houston for over thirty years. She is a loving wife, mother, and grandmother. Sylvia has over thirty-five years experience in Corporate America where she started her career as a legal secretary, being promoted to a paralegal and then, a project manager. She is the owner and CEO of Sylvia G. Phillips Coaching. Sylvia received her BS in Psychology from Our Lady of the Lake University and studied Mental

Health Counseling at Capella University Graduate School. Sylvia is a Certified John Maxwell Coach as well as a workplace and family mediator. Sylvia has general training in the BackStory Breakthrough Method by Dr. Kirleen Neely, PhD, LPC-S. Sylvia is a motivational speaker that has spoken to groups including Jack and Jill – Humble, Kingwood area, Beauty Beyond Breast Cancer, Fresh Spirit Wellness for Women, Shell Oil Company's Black Network, and Shell Oil Company's Women's organization. Sylvia has chaired and raised money for organizations such as Susan G. Komen Shell event, Charmingly Pink Breast Cancer event, and Fresh Spirit Legacy Event.

## Mia Thomas

Mia has a Bachelor Degree in Sociology from Eastern New Mexico University in Portales, New Mexico and A.A.S Degree in Criminal Justice/Law Enforcement from McLennan Community College in Waco, Texas. She is a Licensed Bail bondsman and has a license in Property and Casualty from the State of Texas. She is the Founder of *Real Talk With Real Women* social group that empowers, equip, and bring unity among women of all ages, from various backgrounds and races. She has created a workbook called It's Time to Create, helps people reach their short and long-term goals. She is also the Author of the book called *The Steps of a Real Woman "From Harm to Hurt to Hustle."* Mia is a Certified Life Coach, and has been featured on KWTX New 10-Waco Texas, Moms Everyday show, KXXV news channel and WCCC.TV The Waco City Cable Channel talk show with The Centex African - American Chamber of Commerce and The Cen-Tex Hispanic Chamber of Commerce and appeared in news articles of Waco Tribune Herald and The Anchor Newspaper in Waco, Texas.

## Brittany Hatcher

Brittany Hatcher was born in Fort Worth, Texas and attended all Fort Worth schools before traveling to Tyler, TX for undergraduate studies. Always interested in science, she thought for a second she would study medicine at Texas College. Her thoughts quickly changed when she learned she had to be smothered by a lab coat most days. Still, she majored in Biology and wasn't quite sure what would become of it but knew opportunity would become available once the paper was in hand. Upon graduation Ms. Hatcher returned to Fort Worth to work in three roles at the University of North Texas Health Science Center. Her love for outreach, linking students to their passions and a liaison led her to several roles supporting families within the Fort Worth Independent School District. That same love for other families thrust her to embark leave FWISD full-time to spend more time with her own children. Now, a single mother to 15-year old Kameron and 10-year old Kobin, Ms. Hatcher enjoys managing her full time clothing resale business – Cute Case Resale, acting as a taxi cab for her sports-inspired children and planning her next business ventures.

## Janet Yarbrough

Janet earned a Bachelor's degree in Psychology from UCLA, a Master in Public Administration from California State University Dominguez Hills, and a Certificate of Advanced Professional Development from California State University Northridge. Janet was initiated into Alpha Kappa Alpha Sorority Incorporated in May 1990 and is a life member of the organization.After working nearly thirty years for the County of Los Angeles - primarily in management positions, she retired early so that she could spend more time with her children and to pursue other dreams. She supplements her retirement income by working as an Independent Contractor performing jobs that allow her the flexibility to enjoy life while she waits to see what God has in store for her next. As a widow, she is the proud and devoted mother of two teenage sons, Jonathan and Jared.